GAME CHANGERS
The Greatest Plays in
Philadelphia Eagles
Football History

Reuben Frank and Mark Eckel

TRIUMPH
BOOKS

Library of Congress Cataloging-in-Publication Data

Frank, Reuben.
  Game changers : the greatest plays in Philadelphia Eagles football history / Reuben Frank and Mark Eckel.
      p. cm.
   ISBN 978-1-60078-274-9
   1. Philadelphia Eagles (Football team)—History. I. Eckel, Mark. II. Title.
   GV956.P44F73 2009
   796.332'640974811—dc22

                                                                              2009020090

This book is available in quantity at special discounts for your group or organization. For further information, contact:
   Triumph Books
   542 South Dearborn Street
   Suite 750
   Chicago, Illinois 60605
   (312) 939-3330
   Fax (312) 663-3557
   www.triumphbooks.com

Printed in China
ISBN: 978-1-60078-274-9
Design by Sue Knopf/Patricia Frey
Page production by Patricia Frey
Photographs on pages xiii (top), 25, 33, 67, 85, 93, 99, 112, 117, 119, 125, 131, 141, 209, 210, 228, 299, 334, and 355 courtesy of AP Images. All other photographs courtesy of Getty Images.

*This book is dedicated to the memories of
Jerome Brown, Andre Waters, and Reggie White.*

Contents

Acknowledgments

Without the generous assistance of a number of people, this project would not have been possible. Mark and Reuben would like to thank Adam Motin at Triumph Books for helping us make this the book it needed to be. Thank you Ray Didinger for your invaluable input every step of the way. Thanks to Derek Boyko, Ryan Nissan, Bob Lange, and Brett Strohsacker of the Eagles' public relations department and Eagles video director Mike Dougherty for giving us a glimpse inside his vast archives. And thanks to Merrill Reese, Jim Solano, Rich Burg, Nate Aldsworth, Gary Myers, Andy Schwartz, and Gordon Jones for their suggestions and contributions.

And a very special thanks to the current and former Eagles players and coaches who gave generously of their time and memories: Eric Allen, Fred Barnett, Chuck Bednarik, Bill Bergey, Bill Bradley, Sheldon Brown, Correll Buckhalter, Harold Carmichael, Brad Childress, Garry Cobb, Randall Cunningham, Brian Dawkins, Ted Dean, Hugh Douglas, Tony Franklin, Joselio Hanson, John Harbaugh, Andy Harmon, Al Harris, Artis Hicks, Wes Hopkins, Seth Joyner, Sean Landeta, Chad Lewis, Greg Lewis, Tommy McDonald, Donovan McNabb, Quintin Mikell, Freddie Mitchell, Wilbert Montgomery, Damon Moore, Vince Papale, Andy Reid, Ike Reese, Jon Runyan, Buddy Ryan, Lito Sheppard, Vai Sikahema, Clyde Simmons, Duce Staley, Bobby Taylor, William Thomas, Dick Vermeil, Troy Vincent, Brian Westbrook, Calvin Williams, James Willis, Al Wistert, and Michael Zordich. And a special thanks to Troy Aikman, Tiki Barber, and Carl Banks.

Mark would like to thank his father, Mike, and uncle, Joe, whose endless debates over great plays and great players helped form his opinions at an early age. He would also like to thank Jim Gauger for giving him a chance to witness most of these plays. And his daughter, Erica, who will eventually go on to be a part of the greatest plays in Eckel history.

Reuben thanks Wayne Richardson and the *Burlington County Times* sports staff—you're all pros. He would also like to thank his parents, Morton and Libby Frank, who no doubt will be prominently profiled when somebody writes a book on the 50 Greatest Parents in History. And most of all, he would like to thank his beautiful family: wife, Cindy DeSau, and daughter, Stephanie Frank, for their love, encouragement, and support.

Foreword

It was my distinct honor and privilege to play most of my 13-year NFL career with the Philadelphia Eagles. Becoming a professional football player had been a dream for me since childhood, and it certainly came at a price and with many challenges to overcome. For starters, being drafted in the eighth round, I was not expected to make the team, let alone become a starter, a three-time Pro Bowl player, and a Super Bowl champion. After being cut for the first two games of my rookie year, I returned in Week 3 and was resolute and determined to do whatever was necessary to be a permanent member of the Philadelphia Eagles.

Being a part of a Buddy Ryan team and defense was a unique and special opportunity. As a young team, we grew up in the game together, learned together how to win and play for one goal, and also brought winning and excitement about Eagles football back to the city of Philadelphia. There was a bond, a brotherhood if you will, on this team. Buddy did all he could to impress upon us the importance of being a close-knit family, to keep our business in-house and to be each other's keepers. To fight one of us meant fighting 11 of us, on and off the field. This, I believe, was the key to our success. We ate together, hung out and partied together, and genuinely enjoyed being around each other. This type of unity is rarely seen in professional sports.

Buddy's closeness to us as players caused many problems between him, team management, and owner Norman Braman. During the strike of 1987, while various players from other teams crossed picket lines and played with scabs to replace us, Buddy drew us even closer together, gaining an even deeper respect and loyalty from his players by instructing us as a team to stay unified, to either cross the line together or strike together as a team, knowing we would not cross. He was aware of the discord and conflict that some of us striking and some of us crossing the picket lines would cause us as a team in the long term. This pissed off Braman to no end and was the beginning of the us-against-the-world mantra.

So the clock began ticking on Buddy's days as head coach in Philly. And after playoff losses in 1988, 1989, and 1990, Braman fired Buddy, and that was the beginning of the end of that Eagles era. There was intense frustration and resentment that a coach who put together a team that was second only to the San Francisco 49ers in wins over that three-year period would be fired. We were close to being a Super Bowl contender but would never have the opportunity to realize that potential, especially after the season-ending injury to Randall Cunningham in 1991. The hiring of Rich Kotite—along with our disloyalty to him and the reality that we were not going to be a better team under his leadership—and the untimely death of Jerome Brown in the off-season of 1992 began the dismantling of, in my opinion, one of the greatest defenses in the history of the NFL (although I am a bit biased). First, Keith Jackson left for Miami. Then Reggie departed for Green Bay, Clyde Simmons and I left for Arizona, and Eric Allen finished the exodus by going down to New Orleans. Add in the career-ending injury to Byron Evans, and the Eagles were a mere shell of what we had once been.

I reflect often upon some of the great plays that I had the privilege to watch my teammates make. Randall Cunningham avoiding a cut tackle by Carl Banks and throwing a bullet to Jimmie Giles for a TD. Mike Quick's graceful and acrobatic TD catches. Keith Byars running out of his shoe but never breaking stride, and the crushing block he put on Pepper Johnson, his college roommate, proving without a doubt where his allegiance lay and what he'd do to win. Keith Jackson up the seam against Cover 2, knowing there wasn't a linebacker in the league that could run with him, except me! Jerome Brown looking up at the Jumbotron to see where the offensive pursuer was, en route to a touchdown. B&E doing his *Q* dance after an interception return for a TD. EA's 94-yard scramble back and forth across the field for a touchdown. Clyde Simmons' 4½-sack performance against the Cowgirls in Texas Stadium. Wes Hopkins' nose-shattering forearm to Ernest Givins on *Monday Night Football*. The crazy antics of Andre Waters, "the Dre Masta"— he'd do anything to win, and I never saw a player give his body up like Dre would for the team. And lastly, "the Body Bag Game." I still get chills whenever I watch that game. It was one of the most dominating defensive performances ever.

Seth Joyner

Although many of us finished our careers in other cities, I know we all see ourselves as Eagles for life. It was an honor to retire as an Eagle. Those years flew by like days, and it's hard to believe that this season will mark 10 years of retirement for me. I am eternally grateful to the best fans in the NFL, bar none. They welcomed me with open arms and appreciated the fact that, week in and week out, I tried to give them the best I had to give. They made me a better player. To this day I appreciate the love and respect that I receive still from the City of Brotherly Love. Thank you, Philadelphia!

Seth Joyner
Philadelphia Eagles (1986–1993)

50

September 19, 1976

A Real-Life Rocky

Storybook Hero Papale Forces Fumble, Helps Eagles Win Home Opener vs. Giants

Philadelphia in 1976 was about the bicentennial, Legionnaire's Disease, and *Rocky*. And as Sylvester Stallone created an unforgettable Hollywood hero, a real-life Rocky emerged in Vince Papale. It was only fitting that it happened in Philadelphia. Papale literally came out of the stands and onto the field for the Eagles.

"Dick [Vermeil] had just come in, and did this PR stunt," veteran safety Bill Bradley said. "He had over 150 guys come off the street and try out for the team. Vince really stood out, though.

"He came in that year and he made the team. I mean, he worked his tail off and made it. They didn't hand it to him. He was a special teams guy and a backup receiver. And all I know is, in practice he made the DBs work. He got us ready for Sunday."

Papale was a conference pole vault champion at St. Joseph's University, and he didn't play college football. But he was a pretty good receiver for the Philadelphia Bell of the long-forgotten World Football League. He also played in semi-pro leagues and in some rough-touch games in the vacant lots of South Philadelphia.

"We wrote stories about Vince every day in training camp," said Ray Didinger, then the beat writer for the *Philadelphia Bulletin*. "He was a daily sidebar, but it was such a good story, you had to write it."

As training camp wore on through the summer days, Papale became more than just a hot story. The guy really could play. He led the team in receptions during the preseason games and showed what he could do on special teams with play after key play.

"We would have been surprised if he didn't make it," Didinger said. "If you can get the past the fact he was 30 years old and had never played college ball, it wasn't a surprise."

Vermeil, who took the gamble on the 30-year-old rookie, says even today he wasn't just trying to stir interest in a team that needed to be shaken.

"It wasn't a publicity stunt or anything like that," Vermeil said. "We brought him in because we thought he could help us on special teams, and he did."

Never more so than in his first home game at Veterans Stadium. The Eagles were blown out in the 1976 season opener at Dallas, 27–7, and Papale didn't garner any Rookie of the Year award votes in that one.

"I wanted to redeem myself for what Dick [Vermeil] told me was not a good game against Dallas," Papale recalled. "I got knocked around pretty good in that one. I got hit so hard on one play, I thought I had vertigo.

"Now, we were playing at home. I was juiced up. All my boys were in the stands, all the guys from the neighborhood. The guys I used to sit and watch the game with were there watching me. My dad was there. It was a pretty emotional day for me."

And it got better. The Eagles built a 13–0 lead, but in the fourth quarter the Giants were about to get the ball back. Papale was on the punt team.

"It was late in the game, and we're protecting a slight lead," he said. "They were double-teaming me, just like they did almost the entire game. I had two guys over the top, and that's where the white knuckles from the movie came into play.

Vince Papale looks to engage Patriots special teamer Prentice McCray during a game at Schaefer Stadium in Foxboro, Mass. Vince Papale became a folk hero in Philadelphia during the late 1970s after making the Eagles' roster as a 30-year-old rookie who never played college football.

Invincible

It began in 2001 as a brief clip on a Sunday pregame football show. By 2006, it had turned into one of the most inspirational sports movies ever made.

"NFL Films did a piece on me to celebrate the 25th anniversary of *Rocky*," said Vince Papale. "They did a little feature on the ESPN pregame show."

One thing led to another, a guy from here called a guy from there, and the next thing Papale knew, he was on the phone with people in Hollywood.

"They wanted to know if I was OK with them making a movie about my life," he said. "Of course, I said yes."

The next thing you know, *Invincible*—starring Mark Wahlberg as Vince, Greg Kinnear as Dick Vermeil, and Elisabeth Banks as Janet, Vince's future wife—became a smash hit. Although the filmmakers took some liberties with the facts (for example, Papale had actually played for the Philadelphia Bell of the old World Football League and wasn't a complete football novice), Papale said about 80 percent of the film accurately portrayed his against-all-odds bid to make the Eagles in 1976 as a 30-year-old rookie who had never played college football.

"It was weird," he said, "It still is. I'm still not sure what all the excitement is about. I was on the set every day and watched them film all the scenes and it was strange. It didn't really hit me until the end when they show the film of the play against the Giants."

> There I was on the same field where I grew up watching my heroes play for the past 10 years. In all reality, it doesn't get any better than that.
> —VINCE PAPALE

"I always looked at the guy's hands. If his hands were in the ground to the point where his knuckles were white, I knew he was coming. I looked and I didn't see white knuckles, so I knew he wasn't charging. That gave me the advantage. I was able to split the double team and was the first one downfield.

"Jimmy Robinson was the Giants return man, and I ran his blocker right into him. He hit him, and the ball popped out and went right into my hands. It was crazy. I ran into the end zone and that's the scene you see at the end of the movie. But, of course, you can't return a muff. So we got the ball at around the 9-yard line and scored from there to put the game away."

Papale feels that play finally made him a part of the team. "That's when I finally got accepted," he said. "I went to my first team party after that game. There I was having beers with the guys I used to sit in the stands and cheer— Bill Bergey, Jerry Sisemore, Harold Carmichael, Frank LeMaster. Those guys were my heroes, and now they were my teammates."

Game Details

Philadelphia Eagles 20 • New York Giants 7

Eagles	0	10	3	7	**20**
Giants	0	0	0	7	**7**

Date: September 19, 1976

Team Records: Philadelphia 0–1, New York 0–1

Scoring Plays:

PHI —Carmichael 21-yard pass from Boryla (Muhlmann PAT)

PHI—Muhlmann 44-yard FG

PHI—Muhlmann 38-yard FG

PHI—Boryla 1-yard run (Muhlmann PAT)

NYG—Gillette 7-yard pass from Morton (Danelo PAT)

49

December 18, 1988

O'Brien to Toon

Ken O'Brien of the New York Jets, who would eventually become an Eagle, inadvertently helped his future team win the NFC East when the Jets beat the Giants in a December 1988 game.

The 1988 Eagles are the only team in NFL history to celebrate a division title while gathered around a telephone on the sidelines of an empty stadium.

The Eagles had beaten the Cowboys 23–7 to finish the regular season. But only when the Saints rallied to beat the Falcons did they clinch a playoff berth, and they still needed the Jets to upset the Giants to win the NFC East.

"We never did anything the easy way," head coach Buddy Ryan said. "The tougher it was, the more we liked it."

The Giants led 21–20 late in the fourth quarter, but the Jets, with no postseason to play for, had one last chance.

Eagles broadcaster Merrill Reese stayed on the air and provided Jets-Giants play-by-play to the fans back home. The Philadelphia players remained on the Texas Stadium sideline, where public relations intern Rich Burg passed along updates from team official Jim Gallagher, who was watching the game in the press box.

When Jets quarterback (and future Eagle) Ken O'Brien connected with wide receiver Al Toon on a five-yard touchdown pass with 37 seconds left, Burg barked out the news.

"I said, 'Touchdown Jets,' and helmets went flying. Everybody started hugging each other, and they all ran inside to celebrate," Burg said.

The Jets won 27–21, and the Eagles were NFC champions for the first time in eight years.

"None of it made any sense at the time," Mike Quick said. "I'm just glad we won, the Giants lost, and we won the division."

48

December 28, 2008

Miracle Afternoon

The day began with the Eagles facing an 8 percent chance to reach the playoffs. It ended with backup cornerback Joselio Hanson sprinting triumphantly down the right sideline with one of the longest fumble returns in NFL history, a playoff berth now locked up.

Thanks to the Raiders' upset of the Buccaneers and the Texans' comeback win over the Bears earlier in the day, the Eagles went into the 2008 regular-season finale against the Cowboys needing only a win to reach the playoffs.

"We turned off the TVs in the locker room because we needed the guys to forget everything else and just focus on the Cowboys," head coach Andy Reid said. "But we could all hear the roar of the crowd. We knew something pretty good was happening."

When safety Brian Dawkins stripped the ball from Cowboys running back Marion Barber near the sideline, the ball somehow stayed in bounds and bounced to Hanson, whose 96-yard touchdown return was the longest ever against the Cowboys and 11th-longest in NFL history. The Eagles won 44–6, clinching their seventh playoff berth in nine years.

"It was perfect," Hanson said. "Nine out of 10 times, the ball would go out of bounds. I've never seen a fumble stay in bounds like that. Once I picked up the ball, it was pretty easy: just run.

"A lot had to go right for us that day. Whatever happened, we wanted to beat the Cowboys. As it turned out, everything went our way. It felt like a miracle."

Marion Barber fumbled the ball as he was hit by Brian Dawkins on December 28, 2008. Joselio Hanson recovered the ball and ran it for a touchdown.

47

January 3, 1993

Breaking the Ice

This was the Eagles' fourth trip to the playoffs in five years, and just as in postseason losses to by the Bears, Rams, and Redskins, things looked bleak.

"We needed to win a playoff game," Randall Cunningham said.

The Saints, who had led by as many as 13 points, held a 20–10 lead early in the fourth quarter of their 1992 wild-card game at a revved-up Superdome.

"It looked like it was going to be a bad day," Cunningham said. "I remember it being really loud in the Superdome, and maybe that was bothering us. I don't know. We just couldn't seem to get untracked."

Finally, Cunningham connected with wide receiver Fred Barnett on a 35-yard touchdown pass. The Eagles were back in it.

"I ran a post route, which was supposed to clear things out," Barnett said. "To this day, I don't know why he threw me the ball. I was in double coverage. I looked up and the ball was in the air.

"But that was Randall. He put it in the perfect spot. Any other spot, and it either gets picked off or the corner at least breaks it up. But he put it where only I could get it. One thing about Randall, he always believed in me."

The Eagles outscored the Saints 26–0 in the fourth quarter and won 36–20, their first playoff victory in 12 years.

"That play got us going," Cunningham said. "All of a sudden the dome got real quiet after that. You could tell we turned the momentum."

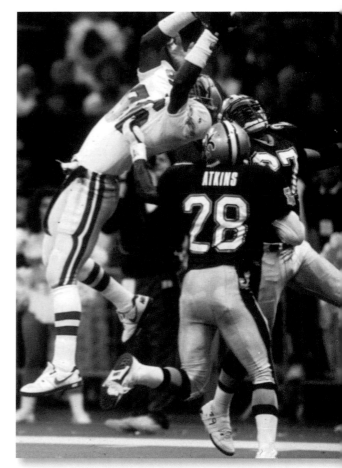

Fred Barnett's 35-yard touchdown catch ignited a 26-point fourth quarter rally that propelled the Eagles to a 36-20 win over the New Orleans Saints in the 1992 NFC Wild Card game.

 **46**

January 19, 2003

Duuuuuuuuuce!

Staley TD Gives Eagles Early Lead vs. Bucs Before NFC Title Game Collapse

When he scored just 52 seconds into the game, there was no doubt in Duce Staley's mind what was happening. "I thought the game was over," Staley says now. "There was no doubt in my mind we were going to the Super Bowl."

Everything was going the Eagles' way in the 2002 NFC Championship Game.

It was the last game ever at decrepit-but-beloved Veterans Stadium. The weather was brutally cold, and the Buccaneers were 1–21 in franchise history with temperatures below 40 degrees. And the Bucs were 0–6 all-time in road playoff games.

The game plan was simple. Pound the undersized Tampa defense all day with Staley. The running back had rushed for 152 yards when the two teams met at the Vet in October, and the Eagles won 20–10. Do it again, and they'd be in their first Super Bowl in 22 years.

"I felt like they couldn't stop me," Staley said. "That wasn't a real big defense. They were quick, but we wanted to run right at them."

And that's what Staley did on his first carry. Brian Mitchell's franchise postseason-record 70-yard return of Martin Gramatica's opening kickoff gave the Eagles the ball at the Tampa 26, and after Staley gained six yards on a pass from Donovan McNabb, he got his first carry of the game on second down. Twenty yards later, the Eagles led 7–0.

"The crowd was going crazy," defensive end Hugh Douglas said. "I thought it would be that way all day long."

Duce Staley scores the first touchdown of the NFC Championship Game against the Tampa Bay Buccanneers at Veterans Stadium on January 19, 2003.

The Vet

It was a dream come true. John Harbaugh had just been named special teams coach of the Eagles, his first NFL coaching job. He was so excited that just before midnight, he drove from his airport hotel up Interstate 95 to Veterans Stadium to check out his new office.

"I was the only one in the building," Harbaugh recalled. "I'm in my office, and, all of a sudden, I hear this scratching sound above me. I thought somebody was trying to break in. I didn't know what it was. It was dark, it was cold. *OK, what's going on?* Just then, a dead bird falls onto my desk. Welcome to Philly. Welcome to the NFL."

Such was life at the Vet, the decrepit, filthy, crumbling, concrete hulk that the Eagles called home from 1971 until the state-of-the-art NovaCare Complex opened across the street in 2001.

But as nasty as the Vet was for the home team, it was worse for the visitors.

"It seemed like it was always cold and damp and dreary there," Troy Aikman said. "We never seemed to play there early in the season when it was warm and the sun was out and it was a beautiful day. It was always dark and cold and the fans were angry about something.

"I played in three Super Bowls, but when I think back, those games against the Eagles at the Vet, those are some of my most vivid memories. I always felt like if I could play at the Vet, I could play anywhere."

Center Hank Fraley and right guard Jermane Mayberry opened up a huge hole for Staley, who powered straight ahead, then made a slight cut to the right at the 10-yard line to elude safety Dexter Jackson and find his way into the end zone.

"The play was 94 weak—I'll never forget it," Staley said. "The hole was huge. The jubilation I felt on the way to the end zone? The excitement I felt? I can't even describe it. It was the loudest I've ever heard that stadium."

Staley's TD run was the longest for the Eagles in the play-offs since Wilbert Montgomery's 42-yarder into the opposite end zone in the NFC championship game 22 years earlier. That one sent the Eagles to the Super Bowl, and everybody felt this one would, too.

"I thought it was history repeating itself," said Montgomery, who served as the Eagles' honorary captain that day. "The feeling was exactly the same. It was a cold day, the crowd was unbelievably loud. Early in the game, the similarities were unbelievable, and I thought the result would be, too."

Game Details

Tampa Bay Buccaneers 27 • Philadelphia Eagles 10

Buccaneers	10	7	3	7	**27**
Eagles	7	3	0	0	**10**

Date: January 19, 2003

Team Records: Philadelphia 12–4, Tampa Bay 12–4

Scoring Plays:

PHI—Staley 20-yard run (Akers PAT)

TB—Gramatica 48-yard FG

TB—Alstott 1-yard run (Gramatica PAT)

PHI—Akers 30-yard FG

TB—K. Johnson 9-yard pass from B. Johnson (Gramatica PAT)

TB—Gramatica 27-yard FG

TB—Barber 92-yard interception return (Gramatica PAT)

Moments later, the Eagles ran out to kick off, and the crowd was still so frenzied kicker that David Akers had to pause so his teammates could settle down.

"I literally thought I was about to have a heart attack on the field," Ike Reese said. "To score that fast? At home? Last game at the Vet? It was too much. I had to tell Akers, 'Dude, let the clock run a little bit before you go ahead and kick the football, so I don't die on the way down the field covering this kick.'"

The feeling was unforgettable. And it was temporary. Head coach Andy Reid quickly abandoned the running game that had the Buccaneers on their heels in the game's opening minute and called 50 pass plays and just 17 runs the rest of the game. Staley, unstoppable on his electrifying TD run, touched the ball on only three of the next 19 snaps and got only 12 carries the rest of the game.

"I just remember standing on the sidelines and being down," Staley said. "I wasn't mad, just down. I had the feeling I could have done so much more."

The Eagles managed only a second-quarter field goal the rest of the way, failed to score on their last nine drives and lost 27–10, the second of their three consecutive NFC Championship Game defeats. The Bucs went on to the Super Bowl in San Diego and battered the Raiders, 48–21.

"The Super Bowl was on the line and I wanted that game on my shoulders," Staley said. "I know if we would have run the ball more, we would have won. And we knew that if we beat Tampa, we would have brutalized Oakland, just like Tampa did."

The 17-point defeat stands as the Eagles' worst ever at home in the postseason and it remains one of the lowest points in franchise history. Although, the first few minutes were among the most thrilling.

"As that game went on, you could just see the momentum was dying," Reese said. "The offense looked out of sync, we weren't running the ball, Donovan didn't look good, and we weren't pounding them. Then they started to pound *us*. To go from that high to where you can't even breathe because you're overwhelmed with excitement, to feel like at end of the game you're at a funeral? That was rough. It was like slow death."

Eagles head coach Andy Reid depended heavily on runners like Duce Staley to round out the Eagles potent offensive attack.

The feeling was unbelievable. We're going to rip out some seats at the Vet and go to the Super Bowl.

—EAGLES TIGHT END CHAD LEWIS

45

November 12, 1979

Good from 59 Yards

Rookie Tony Franklin had already missed two field goal attempts. Now, the Eagles were driving again, hoping to take control of their 1979 game at Texas Stadium.

On third-and-10 from the 42-yard line, Ron Jaworski threw incomplete, and there was also a penalty on the Eagles. Cowboys coach Tom Landry declined the penalty, setting up an Eagles punt. At least, that's what he thought.

"I told Dick I thought I could try it, and Dick yelled, 'Field goal team,'" Franklin says now. "I went out there. I made sure I was set and was able to get some strength behind the kick."

Franklin's career long was a 51-yarder, which he had made just four weeks earlier. This one would be 59 yards. There had only been one field goal that long in NFL history.

"I had hit them that far in practice and during warm-ups," he said. "It was near the end of the half, too, so it was worth taking a shot. As the ball got closer to the goal post, I just waited to see what the official was going to do. When he raised his hands, I jumped in the air."

The Eagles went on to win 31–21, their first win in Dallas after 13 straight losses. Franklin's 59-yard field goal is still the seventh-longest in NFL history.

"I grew up in Fort Worth, so it was nice doing it in Texas Stadium," Franklin said. "My mom and dad were there, my wife—who wasn't my wife yet—was there. It's something I'll never forget."

Tony Franklin and quarterback and holder Ron Jaworski watch the football clear the uprights in one of Franklin's big kicks against the Dallas Cowboys during his career in Philadelphia.

44

January 18, 2009

Ten Minutes from a Super Bowl

DeSean Jackson caught the biggest pass of his life at the 12-yard line. And the 10-yard line. And the 7-yard line. And then twice at the 3-yard line.

It was the fourth quarter of the 2008 NFC championship game in Glendale, Arizona, and Donovan McNabb's bomb down the right sideline was tipped by Cards cornerback Dominique Rodgers-Cromartie, then bounced up off Jackson's hands five times as he ran toward the end zone.

"The ball looked like a hot potato," Cards cornerback Matt Ware said.

The ball finally secure, Jackson had a 62-yard touchdown that gave the Eagles a 25–24 lead.

"I never thought he'd catch it," Rodgers-Cromartie said. "I figured it was going to hit the ground. But he showed great concentration and focus. He kept his eye on it and brought it in. It was a great play."

Jackson's touchdown was the second-longest in NFL postseason history by a rookie, the longest in 35 years.

"I just tried to put it out there for him, and he did a great job of being able to create separation," McNabb said. "Rodgers Cromartie did a great job of catching up to the ball, but that play was really DeSean being able to bring the catch down."

The Eagles were just 10 minutes from their second Super Bowl in five years, a dream that died when Kurt Warner's fourth TD pass gave the Cards a 32–25 win.

"I've seen guys bat a ball up in the air once or maybe twice," Ware said. "But four or five times? It was an amazing play."

DeSean Jackson celebrates his 62-yard touchdown in the second half of the NFC Championship Game against the Arizona Cardinals on January 18, 2009.

43

December 30, 2001

Demo Saves the Day

Moore Races Across Field to Make Season-Saving Tackle at 4-Yard Line

The Eagles were so close to disaster that one day later they still weren't sure how they averted it. "Here's how close it was," Ike Reese said. "We wanted to see it the next day in meetings. We still didn't believe he didn't get in."

All the Eagles needed to beat the Giants and lock up the NFC East title was to make sure the Giants didn't go 80 yards on the final play of the game.

They went 76.

"Honest to God, I'm watching the play thinking, *We are going to be watching this on ESPN Classic for the rest of our lives*," said John Harbaugh, then the Eagles' special teams coach.

Thanks to Donovan McNabb's touchdown pass to Chad Lewis, a quick defensive stop, and then a David Akers field goal with seven seconds remaining, the Eagles had come back from a 21–14 deficit with less than two minutes left to take a 24–21 lead over the Giants late in the 2001 season.

A win would give the Eagles their first division title since 1988. A loss would mean they'd have to win a week later in Tampa, where the Buccaneers were 5–2, to assure themselves of the NFC East crown.

With seven seconds left and 80 yards to go, the Giants were on their own 20. "Honestly? I thought we had it in the bag," safety Damon Moore said.

The Giants needed a miracle, and they almost got it with a play called the Lambuth Special, named after the alma mater of speedy second-year wide receiver Ron Dixon. Quarterback Kerry Collins dropped back, paused, then threw over the middle to All-Pro tailback Tiki Barber, the Giants' most dangerous player.

"It was supposed to be a hook and lateral to Ike [Hilliard], where he pitches it to me and I pitch it to Ron Dixon, but Ike wasn't open," Barber said. "It was really a busted play. All of a sudden, I hear Kerry yelling, 'Tiki! Tiki!' So I turn around and he throws it to me."

Barber caught the ball at the 32-yard line, ran to the 37, stopped abruptly, turned to his right, and flipped the ball to Dixon, who was dashing across the field just behind him. With the Eagles focused on Barber, nobody had accounted for Dixon. He began motoring down the left sideline as time expired.

"I see everybody surrounding Tiki, and then I see this little blur," Moore said. "My heart started to race."

Dixon sprinted to the 40. To midfield. Into Eagles territory. Nobody was close, and he had a wall of blockers lined up to his right.

"You could see everything developing in slow motion," said Reese, who watched from the far sideline. "You could see they had the blocks set up perfectly. When he pitched it to Ron Dixon, I looked immediately at the end zone to see if we had people down there. Because then you say, 'OK, he's going to run around a little bit and then we'll get him.' But we didn't have anybody down there. I couldn't believe it."

Dixon, who a year earlier had opened a playoff win against the Eagles with a 97-yard kickoff return for a touchdown, was about to break their hearts again.

But the cavalry was coming. Moore and cornerback Bobby Taylor were sprinting desperately across the field at an angle, trying to reach Dixon before he reached the end zone.

"Dixon had broken our backs in that playoff game the year before, so I knew how fast he was," Moore said. "I wasn't even thinking about catching anybody, I was just running as fast as I could. It got real quiet. I didn't know if I was going to get there."

Dixon saw only the end zone. "I thought, *I'm going to get in*," he said. "I really thought I was going to get in."

Taylor had a shot at Dixon, but was blocked out of the play by Joe Jurevicius, leaving only Moore with a chance to save the season.

Moore ran through an opening in the traffic that miraculously materialized near the 20-yard line and gave him a route to the sideline. He caught the speeding Dixon at the 12-yard line, dove, and finally brought him down at the 4.

When Damon Moore streaked across the field and dragged down the Giants' Tiki Barber in a December 30, 2001 game, it preserved the Eagles' NFC East title that year.

One more second, and we wouldn't have gotten him.
—EAGLES SAFETY DAMON MOORE

Tight end Chad Lewis celebrates a touchdown catch from Donovan McNabb during the Eagles' 24–21 win over the Giants at the Vet in 2001 as linebacker Michael Barrow looks on. The Eagles went to the NFC Championship Game in four of Lewis's five years as a starter.

"It wasn't a good, solid tackle," Moore said. "But it was good enough."

The Giants needed 80 yards. They got 76. Over on the Eagles' sideline, nobody knew if they had won or lost until an official signaled the play dead.

"Can you imagine if he had scored, and we lost our first NFC East title and home-field advantage [in the first round] because of that?" Reese asked.

The Lambuth Special was the longest offensive play the Eagles allowed during the seven years from 2000 through 2006. But it clinched a division title.

"It's not too often that you give up a 76-yard play and a moment later pandemonium breaks out on your sideline," Harbaugh said.

Eagles defensive coordinator Jim Johnson had prepared the team for just this sort of play. But seeing it unfold in real life was a little different. "They didn't score," Taylor said. "But, man, they came close."

> **I**t seemed like that play took about an hour.
> —EAGLES CORNERBACK BOBBY TAYLOR

Game Details

Philadelphia Eagles 24 • New York Giants 21

Eagles	7	0	0	17	**24**
Giants	0	0	10	11	**21**

Date: December 30, 2001

Team Records: Philadelphia 9–5, New York 7–7

Scoring Plays:

PHI—C. Lewis 5-yard pass from McNabb (Akers PAT)

NYG—Toomer 60-yard pass from Collins (Andersen PAT)

NYG—Andersen 25-yard FG

PHI—Thrash 57-yard pass from McNabb (Akers PAT)

NYG—Andersen 32-yard FG

NYG—Dayne 16-yard run (Barber run)

PHI—C. Lewis 7-yard pass from McNabb (Akers PAT)

PHI—Akers 35-yard FG

Four Straight Titles

From 1950 to 2000, the Eagles finished atop their division or conference three times. They outdid that in the next four years, winning four consecutive NFC East titles from 2001 through 2004, and going 48–16 during that span. Two of the losses came late in 2004, when head coach Andy Reid played the backups after locking up the No. 1 seed throughout the NFC playoffs.

During that remarkable stretch, the Eagles went 25–7 on the road, 21–3 within the NFC East, and 28–6 in meaningful November and December games.

"Those were just real talented teams with lots of good young players and veterans," Hugh Douglas said. "We had fun. I think that was one of the biggest things. We just went out and loved to play football."

The Eagles reached the NFC Championship Game all four years, going to the Super Bowl in 2004.

"The No. 1 thing we had was team chemistry," tight end Chad Lewis said. "It was a mix of unheralded players and overlooked players and extremely talented players, and every person on those teams gave everything they had. And that created a bond that really helped us win close games and tough games.

"There was a real love for each other, a real unity on that team that is so elusive. Teams are constantly trying to forge team chemistry, and it's tough to do when you have a whole bunch of spoiled millionaires. But we had that, and it's one of the big reasons we won."

42

August 20, 2004

81 for 81

On the first play of his first home game, Terrell Owens gave Eagles fans exactly what they had been waiting for.

"That's what people came out to see," Owens said after catching an 81-yard touchdown pass from Donovan McNabb in a preseason game against the Ravens. "That's what the Eagles brought me here to do, and that's why I wanted to come here and play with No. 5."

It didn't count in the stats. But it sure meant a lot. "That was a statement of what we were going to be all about," McNabb said. "It was like we had arrived."

The Eagles had lost their third straight NFC Championship Game the year before, 14–3 to Carolina. Management knew it had to surround McNabb with more than James Thrash and Todd Pinkston.

Enter Owens.

"Sometimes certain things happen where all of a sudden a team changes," McNabb said. "That's what happened in that Baltimore preseason game. That play showed something we hadn't had in the past."

Five months later, the Eagles reached the Super Bowl. But the magic didn't last. Seven games into 2005, Owens was banished for conduct detrimental to the team.

Though things started off well in training camp for Donovan McNabb and Terrell Owens and continued into the first half of the season, the relationship soon deteriorated as Owens' me-first attitude eventually undermined the team.

"If they kept playing together, they could have been the best ever," head coach Andy Reid said.

Owens caught 133 passes for 2,085 yards and 20 TDs in his 22 games with McNabb.

"There was nothing those two couldn't do," Hugh Douglas said. "If they could have just worked it out, who knows how many games we would have won."

41

January 23, 2005

A Bad Break

As loud as the roar from the crowd was, it wasn't loud enough to drown out the pop Chad Lewis heard in his foot.

"I knew I broke it," Lewis says today. "I knew instantly my season was over, and I knew I wasn't going to the Super Bowl."

Lewis's two-yard touchdown catch from Donovan McNabb with 3:21 left in the 2004 NFC Championship Game at the Linc gave the Eagles a 27–10 lead over the Falcons.

That reception capped a remarkable career for Lewis, who went undrafted out of BYU and was released by two teams before becoming a three-time Pro Bowl tight end with the Eagles. But while coming down with the ball, Lewis had suffered the dreaded lisfranc sprain. He underwent surgery three days later, and after waiting all his life to play in a Super Bowl, he was forced to watch from the sidelines two weeks later when the Eagles lost to the Patriots in Super Bowl XXXIX in Jacksonville.

"At the same moment that I knew my season was over, I also felt an incredible sense of calm and peace in my heart," Lewis said. "I remember thinking about what a privilege it is just getting into the playoffs, that a lot of guys play in the league for a long time and never get to experience that. I had played well in the playoffs and was able to help my team get to the Super Bowl. At that moment, I was thinking, *If you complain now, you're the biggest loser around*."

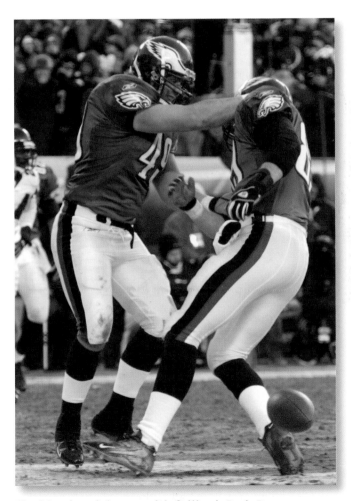

Chad Lewis celebrates with fullback Josh Parry after Lewis scored a touchdown against the Atlanta Falcons in the NFC Championship Game in Philadelphia on January 23, 2005.

40

October 19, 1969

Put Me In, Coach!

After Begging for a Chance, Bradley Returns Staubach Interception for Touchdown in NFL Debut

Five weeks into his rookie season, Bill Bradley had punted, returned punts and kickoffs, and held for field goals and extra points. But what the third-round draft choice out of Texas hadn't done was what he did best: play safety. And it was driving him crazy.

A month into that 1969 season, the Eagles were 1–3 and getting pounded by the Cowboys at the Cotton Bowl. Yet the East Texas native and former University of Texas Longhorn remained glued to the bench while row after row of friends and family watched.

"Dallas was beating us up pretty good," Bradley said. "It's the middle of the third quarter, and Dallas started putting some subs in at that point. [Craig] Morton was out and Roger Staubach, who had just come out of the service at that point, was in the game at quarterback.

"So I go over to our coaches—Jimmy Carr and Joe Moss were the defensive coaches—and I say, 'Hey, they have their subs in the game, why don't you guys put some of our subs in?' Carr turns around and tells me to get away from him. 'Can't you see I'm trying to coach here, Bradley?' he says to me."

Bradley went back to the bench, but when the Cowboys went ahead 42–7, he couldn't take any more. He tried again.

"It's the middle of the fourth quarter, and I go back over to Carr again," he said. "This time he says, 'Aw, hell, just get in the game, Bradley.'"

On his first NFL play from scrimmage, the 22-year-old safety stepped in front of one Hall of Famer and intercepted a pass thrown by another Hall of Famer before nearly getting run down by yet another Hall of Famer.

Staubach was the quarterback, tight end Mike Ditka was the intended receiver, and Olympic sprinter Bob Hayes was the one chasing Bradley a few seconds into his career as an NFL safety.

"I was always a film-study guy, so I was prepared," Bradley said. "Now, they're still beating us pretty good and they have the new quarterback in, so we're blitzing them. We called 'Sticky Sid,' which is an all-out blitz. The strong safety blitzed, the linebackers blitzed, and we're in what they now call 'zero coverage.' I'm the free safety, and I have to cover the tight end, Ditka.

Bill Bradley, who still shares the franchise record with 34 interceptions, drops back in coverage against the Super Bowl-champion Steelers during the Eagles' 27–0 loss at Three Rivers Stadium in Pittsburgh in 1974. Bradley never played on a winning team during his nine years with the Eagles.

"Staubach sees what's coming, and he's looking for his hot read and does a check at the line. Ditka doesn't see it, but I did. Roger checks off and throws to where he thinks Ditka is going to be, but Mike ran straight ahead, and I ran to the spot where he was supposed to be. I caught it at our 44-yard line, juked to the right, zigzagged a little, and went up the sideline to score."

It wasn't quite that easy.

"Well, we're in Texas and I have about 35 people in the stands, friends, guys from high school, some relatives," Bradley recalls today. "So I'm running to the end zone with the ball in one hand and showing the Cowboys' fans my IQ with my other hand.

"Now, keep in mind I wasn't all that fast. Bob Hayes ran a post route on the play and is in the end zone when I catch the ball at the 44. I didn't realize

Bill Bradley

Bill Bradley led the NFL with 11 interceptions in 1971 and figured he deserved a raise. "I figured I was doing five jobs: I was punting, returning punts, returning kickoffs, holding [on kicks], and starting at safety. The average salary back then was anywhere from $15,000 to at the high end maybe $20,000.

"When I went in [before the 1972 season], I told them I'll still do all five jobs, but I wanted $50,000. I thought that was a break for them, because if they got rid of me they would have to sign five players to replace me."

Bradley was only 25, and his 11 interceptions in 1971 were not only a club record but at the time the 11th–highest total in NFL history. But the Eagles weren't impressed with his logic and didn't offer him a raise. So he and linebacker Tim Rossovich, another of the team's talented and colorful players, staged a high-profile holdout while their teammates toiled at training camp.

"We had a great time," Bradley said. "It was like playing cops and robbers. We hid out down the Jersey Shore going from one motel to the next, just to duck people. That was a lot of fun. It was like being in a movie."

The Eagles cut the cast in half when they traded Rossovich to San Diego, leaving Bradley alone in his protest. "Now, I'm by myself and training camp opens at Albright College in Reading," Bradley recalls today. "So I load up my '67 VW bus and meet up with this girl from Reading, Cis Rundle [later a Rams cheerleader and movie star], who used to hang out with us. I park the bus just outside the 50-yard line, and we're making sandwiches and selling them with sodas during camp.

"I'm making $125, $150 bucks a day. That's more than the players on the field were getting, and they're going through two-a-day practices. The players, they loved it. But I was starting to get on management's nerves, I think."

It worked. Bradley got his new deal, a three-year contract averaging a whopping $75,000 per year. It was also loaded with incentives, some of them unusual.

"I had all kinds of clauses," Bradley said. "I put things in there, and I don't even think Mr. Tose [owner Leonard] or Mr. Murray [general manager Jim] even read it. They just wanted to get me out of there and back on the field."

Bradley followed his 11-interception season with nine more in 1972 and became the first player in NFL history to lead the league in interceptions in consecutive seasons. Unfortunately, the Eagles averaged fewer than four wins per season and never reached the playoffs during Bradley's eight years in Philadelphia. He retired after a brief stint with the Cards in 1977.

"We didn't win much," Bradley said. "The best team we had was just .500. But our defense was always solid, and it was a great bunch of people. I loved my time in Philadelphia."

Former Eagles player Bill Bradley smiles at the induction ceremonies at the Texas Sports Hall of Fame on March 4, 2009 in Waco, Texas. He is signing a painting of himself during his college days playing at the University of Texas.

it then, but when I've watched the tape, Bullet Bob Hayes comes out of his end zone and starts sprinting. Nobody blocked him, and he hits me just as I got in the end zone and got called for a 15-yard penalty."

Bradley finished with 34 interceptions to set an Eagles record that was later tied by Eric Allen and Brian Dawkins.

"I've gotten to know Eric Allen over the years, and we've talked about sharing the record," Bradley said. "But shoot, that record has been around since 1977. That might be as long as a record has lasted."

Game Details

Dallas Cowboys 49 • Philadelphia Eagles 14

Cowboys	28	7	7	7	**49**
Eagles	7	0	0	7	**14**

Date: October, 19, 1969
Team Records: Philadelphia 1–3, Dallas 4–0
Scoring Plays:

DAL—Rentzel 9-yard pass from Morton (Clark PAT)
DAL—Rentzel 16-yard pass from Morton (Clark PAT)
PHI—Jackson 65-yard pass from Snead (Baker PAT)
DAL—Lilly 9 yard fumble return (Clark PAT)
DAL—Hayes 67-yard pass from Morton (Clark PAT)
DAL—Rentzel 15-yard pass from Morton (Clark PAT)
DAL—Norman 31-yard pass from Morton (Clark PAT)
PHI—Bradley 56 yard interception return (Baker PAT)
DAL—Reeves 1-yard run (Clark PAT)

That was my first. Who would have ever thought it would end with 34 for the Eagles?

—BILL BRADLEY

39

Gutting It Out

McNabb Overcomes Huge Hits to Keep Super Bowl Alive with TD Pass to Lewis

That summer, six months after the Eagles lost to the Patriots in the Super Bowl, NFL Vice President of Officiating Mike Pereira visited Eagles training camp at Lehigh University. The Eagles were waiting.

They believed the Patriots got away with countless cheap shots on quarterback Donovan McNabb in their 24–21 win over the Eagles in Super Bowl XXXIX in Jacksonville, and now they had the video to prove it.

"At first, he didn't take us seriously," recalls John Harbaugh, then-Eagles special teams coach. "Then we showed him the tape, and he could not believe the shots Donovan took out of bounds and late in that game. Their whole thing was to hit Donovan and hurt him, and that's fine, but it was the officials' job to protect him, and they didn't. Imagine if Tom Brady got hit late that many times? Tell me they wouldn't call those penalties. When you watch that game, and you see the shots Donovan took, it's incredible what he was able to do."

So while many fans have focused on McNabb gasping for air and appearing to throw up in the final moments of the Super Bowl, the reality is that a moment earlier, All-Pro defensive end Richard Seymour demolished McNabb with a devastating hit that nearly knocked him out of the biggest game of his life.

"He got shellacked," head coach Andy Reid said.

Millions of fans saw him doubled over in pain, desperately trying to get the ball snapped before the play clock expired. They had no clue why.

"People always focus on me supposedly throwing up," McNabb says now. "Richard Seymour got me pretty good. I got hit in the face and my helmet went backwards and I had stuff in my face. I'm trying to catch my breath and get my vision back. People make it out like I was tired. I just got killed.

"Nobody focuses on the plays we made, they just talked about, 'Oh, he choked in the Super Bowl.'"

Although McNabb passed for three touchdowns and 357 yards against the Patriots—only Kurt Warner has had more in a Super Bowl—he's remembered more for throwing up in the final minutes than throwing a brilliant touchdown pass.

There's certainly film of the Patriots teeing off on McNabb, especially during the second half, when the Eagles had to throw.

Despite being enveloped and pounded by the New England Patriots' defense for much of the game, Donovan McNabb gutted it out to give the Eagles a shot at victory until late in Super Bowl XXXIX in Jacksonville, Florida, on February 6, 2005.

> **A** few series beforehand, Greg went to Donovan and told him if he ran a double move, he could beat his guy. Donovan listened, and we got a touchdown out of it.
>
> **—EAGLES GUARD ARTIS HICKS**

Game Details

New England Patriots 24 • Philadelphia Eagles 21

Patriots	0	7	7	10	**24**
Eagles	0	7	7	7	**21**

Date: February 6, 2005

Team Records: Philadelphia 13–3, New England 14–2

Scoring Plays:

PHI—Smith 6-yard pass from McNabb (Akers PAT)

NE—Givens 4-yard pass from Brady (Vinatieri PAT)

NE—Vrabel 2-yard pass from Brady (Vinatieri PAT)

PHI—Westbrook 10-yard pass from McNabb (Akers PAT)

NE—Dillon 2-yard run (Vinatieri PAT)

NE—Vinatieri 22-yard FG

PHI—G. Lewis 30-yard pass from McNabb (Akers PAT)

> **P**eople have never given Donovan enough credit for what he accomplished in that game.
>
> **—EAGLES SPECIAL TEAMS COACH JOHN HARBAUGH**

"First play of the game, he scrambled left and got hit pretty good out of bounds—it should have been a late hit, but they didn't call it," said Brad Childress, then the Eagles' offensive coordinator. "That's never a good sign, when your quarterback is getting hit like that on the first play of the game. He got hit a lot, but he continued to hang in there and compete."

Those hits took a brutal toll. "Donovan got battered," receiver Greg Lewis said. "I know he was hurting at the end of the game. But in the huddle, he was his normal self. He was just regular Donovan, running around and trying to make plays."

Whether he threw up or not, McNabb did complete eight of 10 passes for 79 yards on a critical fourth-quarter drive in the final minutes of a Super Bowl. And with 1:55 left in the game and the Patriots leading 24–14, he connected with Lewis on a spectacular 30-yard touchdown pass that brought the Eagles within three points.

"Donovan can put the ball in spots where most quarterbacks can't," Lewis said. "On that touchdown, he just put it up there and gave me a chance to go get it."

McNabb's first read, tight end L.J. Smith, slowed as he ran a crossing route from left to right. McNabb then spotted Lewis running down the middle of the field a step ahead of safety Dexter Reid. He quickly reset his feet and fired, and Lewis soared high in the air, securing the ball with his arms reaching straight up as he crossed over the goal-line.

"Donovan took a beating in that game, but he hung in there, hung in there, hung in there," guard Artis Hicks said. "And eventually, he came up with a big play when we really needed one."

Moments later, McNabb's first Super Bowl appearance was over, and the Patriots had their third NFL championship in four years.

"Yes, we didn't win, we know that," McNabb said. "But we did a lot of positive things that people didn't expect us to do. It wasn't even supposed to be close. We all wanted to win. We just didn't win that night."

Donovan McNabb

Donovan McNabb is one of the most praised athletes in Philadelphia history—and one of the most criticized.

McNabb takes an 82–45–1 regular-season record and 9-6 postseason mark into the 2009 season, despite playing only one of those 15 playoff games with a Pro Bowl receiver.

And yet he finds himself under constant scrutiny. He's not accurate enough. He doesn't scramble enough. He's not a leader. His 1–4 record in NFC title games isn't good enough. You name it, he's heard it.

"If we as a team had won just one championship, they would have given Donovan the keys to the city," said teammate Chad Lewis. "If we had won two, he's in Canton. But when we lost those games, there was so much disappointment and frustration because the fans wanted it so bad that Donovan became the scapegoat."

McNabb has found himself embroiled in controversy since day one with the Eagles, but only seven quarterbacks in NFL history have won more regular-season games with a higher winning percentage, and only seven have won more playoff games.

"I understand you have struggles in this business at the quarterback position. Nobody is immune to it," Kurt Warner said. "But the crazy thing is how many people have doubted him or looked to replace him. To his credit, he stood up with character every time. He's battled through it. He comes back every single time and proves everyone wrong. I just hope, at some point, they start giving him the credit he deserves."

The oft-misunderstood Donovan McNabb does a radio interview on January 30, 2009 in Tampa, Florida.

38

September 10, 1995

A New Era

They had an eight-game losing streak over two seasons. They had lost 21–6 to the Buccaneers on opening day. They had a new head coach. Their Pro-Bowl quarterback had been benched earlier in the game. And all the leaders who had guided them through hard times in previous years—Reggie White, Eric Allen, Seth Joyner—were long gone. The Eagles were in shambles.

"There was a lot going on," said linebacker William Thomas. "There were a lot of unknowns. It was definitely a transition period."

The 1995 Eagles were looking for an identity, looking for hope, looking for a win. And on a Sunday night at Sun Devil Stadium, Thomas made sure they got all of the above.

Thomas intercepted Arizona quarterback Dave Krieg early in the second quarter and returned it 37 yards for a touchdown, the first TD of the Ray Rhodes era. It gave the Eagles a 7–0 lead on the way to a 31–19 win that propelled them to a 10–6 season.

"Whenever I saw a quarterback in a quick three-step drop, I immediately started buzzing toward the flat, because you know it's going to be a quick hitch or a quick slant," said Thomas, the only player in NFL history with at least 25 interceptions and 35 sacks. "I just grabbed the ball and started running. That was my first touchdown, and it got us going. It was still early in the year, but we hadn't won a game in a while and we needed that one."

Linebacker William Thomas returns an interception thrown by Tommy Maddox during the Eagles' 17–14 win over the Giants at the Meadowlands in 1995. Thomas's interception of Cards quarterback David Krieg and 37-yard return for a touchdown five weeks earlier at Sun Devil Stadium ended an eight-game losing streak and gave Ray Rhodes his first win as Eagles head coach.

37

September 23, 1974

Proving He Belongs

Bergey Makes a Statement in His First Game at the Vet

Bill Bergey was still furious at the Bengals. After five outstanding years in Cincinnati, the Bengals refused to give him what he believed was a fair contract, so he demanded a trade and wound up in Philadelphia in the fall of 1974.

His first game in front of the home fans was a Monday night national telecast against the Cowboys. And he had made up his mind to prove that the Bengals goofed when they refused to pay him fairly and to make a good first impression on the Eagles fans who were curious about the middle linebacker who cost them two first-round picks.

"It was on my mind that day that they were going to find out they made a big mistake by getting rid of me," Bergey says of the Bengals. "I was going to play as hard as I could to prove them wrong."

He got his chance very quickly. With the Cowboys already ahead 7–0, Dallas had first-and-goal on the Eagles' 3-yard line. The Eagles held on the first two

The Cincinnati Bengals refused to pay Bill Bergey what he thought he was worth and traded him to the Eagles, where he made a big statement in his first game playing for his new team in 1974.

plays, but on third down, running back Doug Dennison, a rookie from Kutztown State, took a handoff from Roger Staubach and appeared to have an open lane to the end zone to make it a 14–0 lead.

That's when Bergey showed the form that would earn him four Pro Bowl selections in his six seasons in Philadelphia.

"It was just one of those real good hits," Bergey remembers. "I lined him up and hit him, and the ball came loose."

Dennison, who had given the Cowboys a 7–0 lead in the second quarter with a three-yard TD run, fumbled at the 1-yard line and the ball bounced out to the 4, where cornerback Joe Lavender scooped it up.

"I turned and there it was, bouncing along in front of me," Lavender told reporters after the game. "I picked

Safety Randy Logan had a key block on Joe Lavender's 96-yard return of a fumble by Doug Dennison for a touchdown against the Cowboys during a Monday night game at the Vet in 1974. The fumble was forced by Bill Bergey, who was playing in his first home game for the Eagles.

Game Details

Philadelphia Eagles 13 • Dallas Cowboys 10

Eagles	0	0	7	6	**13**
Cowboys	0	7	0	3	**10**

Date: September 23, 1974

Team Records: Philadelphia 0–1, Dallas 1–0

Scoring Plays:

DAL—Dennison 3-yard run (Percival PAT)

PHI—Lavender 96-yard fumble return (Dempsey PAT)

PHI—Dempsey 33-yard FG

DAL—Percival 26-yard FG

PHI—Dempsey 45-yard FG

it up and then it was just a matter of running."

With the help of a block by Randy Logan, Lavender ran 96 yards for a touchdown, at the time the fourth-longest fumble return in NFL history.

"I stumbled but I got my balance right away," he said. "From there, it was just a foot race. I didn't get tired until I crossed the goal line. The thing is, the coaches had been telling us all week to just dive on fumbles and not worry about returning them. Will Wynn had a chance to recover one a couple weeks ago, but he didn't get it because he tried to run with it. All that was going through my mind."

Bergey and Lavender both went on to outstanding careers. Bergey made five Pro Bowl teams in all and All-Pro twice. His 27 interceptions were still ninth-most in NFL history by a linebacker entering 2009. Lavender became a starter with the Redskins and went to two Pro Bowls, finishing his 10-year career with 33 interceptions.

They only played two years together, but they combined on one of the greatest plays in team history.

Cornerback Joe Lavender used his quick hands to scoop up the fumble caused by teammate Bill Bergey and returned the ball 96 yards for an Eagles touchdown.

December 16, 2007

Westbrook Takes a Knee

Brian Westbrook has been pursued throughout his life by linebackers and safeties. This was the first time he was chased down by one of his teammates.

"As a running back, you're taught from the time you start playing to get in the end zone," Westbrook said. "The whole purpose is to try to score."

But late in the fourth quarter of a 10–6 win over the Cowboys in 2007, Westbrook's decision to *not* score clinched a win for the Eagles.

The Eagles led 10–6 when Westbrook took a handoff at the 25-yard-line and broke free.

"In the huddle, Jon [Runyan] said, 'West, if you break one, don't go in. Stop at the 1.' I said, 'Yeah, I know.' But really, I was saying, 'Are you crazy?' The thing about offensive linemen is, the last thing you want to do is piss them off. So I just went along with him."

Then it happened, just as Runyan predicted. "I'm running to the end zone, and just as I look back, I see Jon, and he's yelling, 'Go down, West! Go down!'" Westbrook said. "It was like one of those scenes out of a movie in slow motion, this big man running after me. But I went down at the 1."

Had Westbrook scored, Dallas could have scored, recovered an onside kick, and then scored again. Since the Cowboys had no timeouts, Westbrook's maneuver eliminated their only shot at winning.

"It's pretty simple, really," Runyan said. "If he goes down, the game is over. If he scores, it's not over."

Brian Westbrook takes a knee at the 1-yard line instead of scoring a touchdown against the Dallas Cowboys late in the fourth quarter of the Eagles' win on December 16, 2007.

35

January 13, 2007

Bush Whacked

Sheldon Brown defended the play so much in practice that he grew tired of it. Then he saw it for real and couldn't believe his eyes.

"You don't see that happen too often," Brown recalls. "I said, 'Oh my God, this is exactly how it looked in practice.'"

Early in the Eagles' 2006 playoff game in New Orleans, the Saints ran one of their offensive staples, a swing pass to explosive tailback Reggie Bush.

"They'd been killing everybody with that play," safety Quintin Mikell said. "Sheldon was ready for it. I don't think he even took a step back, he just saw what was coming, went forward, and gave him everything he had."

Bush caught the pass from Drew Brees near the 35-yard line, but before Bush could take a step, Brown blasted into him, separating him from the ball and sending him sprawling to the turf.

"That was a gorgeous hit," Brian Dawkins said. "It may have been the hardest hit I've ever seen."

Bush crawled around for a moment before being helped off the field. He eventually returned and even scored a touchdown. "I couldn't believe he came back in," Eagles radio analyst Mike Quick said. "I would have taken my ball and gone home. And nobody would have complained if I did."

Even though the Saints won, Brown's hit made the cover of *Sports Illustrated* over the headline "Big Hits."

"That was a beastly, beastly hit," Dawkins said. "He just demolished him. I don't know another corner who can destroy somebody like that."

In the first quarter of the Eagles-Saints playoff game in 2006, cornerback Sheldon Brown sniffed out a screen pass to Reggie Bush and flattened the former Heisman Trophy winner with a thunderous hit that Brian Dawkins called "the hardest hit I've ever seen."

34

November 25, 1990

Byars Obliterates His Best Man

Each week, coach Buddy Ryan compiled a videotape with all the massive hits that the Eagles' defensive stars had made in the previous Sunday's game.

"Keith Byars would always talk about how he was going to make a big hit and get on that video," Eric Allen said. "We were like, 'Come on, you're a running back, you're not going to hit anybody.' We just laughed about it."

In 1990, Byars turned in the greatest block in Eagles history. With the Eagles and Giants tied 7–7 at the Vet, Byars spotted his best friend, New York linebacker Pepper Johnson, racing toward a scrambling Randall Cunningham. Byars intercepted Johnson and blind-sided him with a vicious block, knocking him backwards three yards.

"His teammates dogged him out," Byars said. "They said, 'That's your boy. Your boy hit you like that.' We had to call timeout because we had to look at the replay on Diamond Vision."

Cunningham gained 13 yards to set up a touchdown, and the Eagles went on to win, 31–13.

"That shows our mentality toward the game," Johnson said. "Keith wasn't blocking his old college roommate or best man at his wedding. He was trying to win."

That win over the 10–0 Giants helped the Eagles finish 10-6 and reach the playoffs for a third straight year.

"That was one of the greatest blocks I've ever seen," Allen said. "He completely clocked him. I mean, he just *annihilated* him. We all immediately started saying, 'I think Keith is finally going to make the highlight film next week.'"

Keith Byars' crushing block against his friend and fellow Ohio Sate alum, Giants linebacker Pepper Johnson, made coach Buddy Ryan's legendary weekly highlight reel of big hits by the Eagles defense.

33

December 4, 2006

The Good Sheppard

They were 5–6, they had lost Donovan McNabb for the season, and now the Eagles were on the brink of playoff elimination for a second straight year.

The Panthers trailed the Eagles by three but had a first-and-goal on the 7-yard line with 28 seconds left. Quarterback Jake Delhomme slapped his hip, signaling fade pass to Keyshawn Johnson. Lito Sheppard took note.

"I knew right then it was coming," Sheppard said. "Now I had to make a play on it." He timed his jump, leaped, and grabbed Delhomme's pass, somehow managing to keep both feet in bounds in the deep right corner of the end zone for a season-saving interception.

"I just tried to keep Keyshawn in front of me," Sheppard said. "If he got behind me, I knew they would just lob it up there over my head. I just kept saying to myself, *Don't let him get out. Keep him inside.* The pass went just as I hoped."

The Eagles had a 27–24 Monday night win, Jeff Garcia's first as an Eagle.

"That play saved the season for us," Sheldon Brown said. "For him to catch the ball, drag his heel, and get both feet inbounds—that's just crazy."

Garcia then guided the Eagles to four more wins, and the Eagles finished 10–6 and won the 2006 division title, their fifth in six years.

"That season was rough at that point," Sheppard said. "We needed to get something going. We won that game, and it got us on a roll."

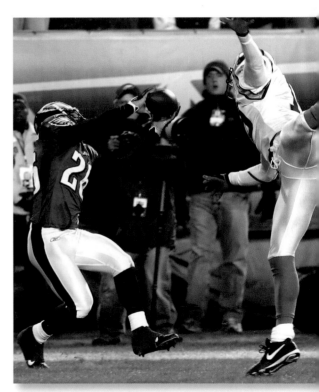

Lito Sheppard intercepts a pass intended for Carolina Panthers wide receiver Keyshawn Johnson with 28 seconds remaining in the fourth quarter of a game on December 4, 2006. The Eagles won 27–24.

32

October 29, 1961

Sure Hands, Sure Touchdown

McDonald's Last-Second TD Catch vs. Redskins Keeps Eagles' Postseason Hopes Alive

Tommy McDonald had just one thing on his mind. "The ball was coming, I was open, and I just kept telling myself, *You better not drop this one, you better not drop this one*,' McDonald said. "I mean, this was the game. We were either going to win or lose on this play."

McDonald didn't drop many in his Hall of Fame career, and he surely didn't drop this one. His 41-yard touchdown catch from Sonny Jurgensen as time expired gave the Eagles a 27–24 win over the Redskins and kept them in the 1961 playoff hunt.

"Washington hadn't been playing well, but they gave us a tough time that day," McDonald said. "Sometimes it's hard to get up for a team when you look at their record. But they were up for us."

Washington was 0–6 and had scored just one touchdown in his last three games going into the matchup at D.C. Stadium. The defending NFL-champion Eagles were 5–1 and had outscored their last two opponents 63–14. But the Redskins took a 24–20 lead with just 50 seconds left

when rookie quarterback Norm Snead threw a seven-yard touchdown pass to fullback Jim Cunningham.

When the Eagles got the ball back, Jurgensen then moved them from their own 20-yard line to the Washington 41 with two passes to Bobby Walston. But time was ticking away as his next pass fell incomplete.

"We had time for one more play, and that was it," McDonald said. "I ran a deep slant pattern, got by the defensive back, and Sonny put it right there for me. All I had to do was catch it."

McDonald almost always caught it. In the 1960 championship season, he scored 13 touchdowns on just 39 receptions. He followed that with his best season, in 1961, when he caught 64 passes for a league-leading 1,144 yards and 13 touchdowns. From 1958 through 1962, he scored 55 touchdowns, second only to Browns all-timer Jim Brown during that time span.

"I would study [defensive backs] on film, and I knew him better than he knew himself sometimes," McDonald said. "Whenever I went out on that field to play, I knew whether I could double-fake him or single-fake him or anything like that. This time I just ran by him. I did what I could do to get in the end zone. That was my job, to get in the end zone, score points."

McDonald went to six Pro Bowls in his career, five of those in seven years for the Eagles.

When San Francisco 49ers cornerback Jimmy Johnson was voted into the Hall of Fame, he was asked who the most difficult receiver he ever faced was. Without pausing, he replied, "Tommy McDonald." Another of the great cornerbacks of that cra, Johnny Sample of the Colts, said McDonald was the only player he ever feared, "Because he never quit, never gave up."

When he retired in 1968, McDonald's 84 touchdown receptions ranked second in NFL history to Green Bay's Don Hutson (99). All these years later, he still ranks 14th, with more TDs than 29 of the 33 other ends and receivers in the Hall of Fame.

"You put his numbers against any receiver of his time and he blows them away," NFL historian Ray Didinger said of McDonald. "He was just an amazing player in terms of big plays."

And then there were his hands. McDonald says he never dropped a pass.

After a memorable college and pro career that included a last-second touchdown catch against the Redskins in October 1961, Tommy McDonald was elected to the Pro Football Hall of Fame on January 24, 1998.

And Didinger, who watched every game he played, confirms it. Never. "My dad was an electrician back in New Mexico and I used to help him," McDonald remembers. "I would put in the receptacles for him, and I would have to screw them in with a screwdriver. It made my wrists and fingers so strong. I always say that's what helped me have such strong hands. It was a blessing in disguise.

"I had a method. Everybody has a method, right? I would never reach out to catch a pass. I would always kind of cradle it into my body and trap it between my forearm and elbow. I never wanted to let a defensive back be able to slap it away."

They never did.

> **I**f I had to pick one guy to throw the ball to with the game on the line, I'd pick Tommy. I knew somehow he'd get open and catch it.
>
> —EAGLES QUARTERBACK NORM VAN BROCKLIN

Game Details

Philadelphia Eagles 27 • Washington Redskins 24

Eagles	7	7	3	10	**27**
Redskins	7	10	0	7	**24**

Date: October 29, 1961

Team Records: Philadelphia 5–1, Washington 0–6

Scoring Plays:

WAS—Horner 3-yard pass from Snead (Aveni PAT)

PHI—Retzlaff 44-yard pass from Jurgensen (Walston PAT)

WAS—Bosseler 3-yard run (Walston PAT)

WAS—Aveni 52-yard FG

PHI—Retzlaff 11-yard pass from Jurgensen (Walston PAT)

PHI—Walston 13-yard FG

PHI—Walston 33-yard FG

WAS—Cunningham 7-yard pass from Snead (Aveni PAT)

PHI—McDonald 41-yard pass from Jurgensen (Walston PAT)

Pete Retzlaff

In 1956, the Detroit Lions got rid of a fullback who had never caught a pass in college or the NFL. He became one of the greatest receivers in NFL history. Eagles head coach Buck Shaw converted Pete Retzlaff to receiver in 1956, and by 1958, Retzlaff led the NFL with 56 receptions for 766 yards. It was just a start. Retzlaff led the Eagles in receptions six times, made five Pro Bowl teams and eventually had his number 44 retired by the team.

When he retired, Retzlaff's 452 receptions and 7,412 yards were first in Eagles history, and his 47 touchdowns were third. Not bad for a converted fullback.

"It's a great honor, it really is," Retzlaff said when his name and number went into the Eagles Honor Roll.

"When you look at the names you're associated with, you can't help but be proud. It puts you in a very special category."

Retzlaff was also very active in early union activities. He was the Eagles' player representative and eventually served as NFLPA president, helping craft the contracts still being used today.

"We wanted a pension program for the players," he told the Eagles' website in 2004. "We wanted health benefits for the players. We wanted it written into the contract that when a player got hurt while performing his duty under the contract, that the club had the responsibility to make sure he was given the proper health care. Some of those things weren't written into the contract then. They are now."

Sonny Jurgensen

When the Eagles traded Sonny Jurgensen to the Redskins for Norm Snead after the 1963 season, it changed the course of two rival franchises for a generation.

After coach Buck Shaw and quarterback Norm Van Brocklin both retired following the Eagles' 1960 NFL Championship Game win, Nick Skorich replaced Shaw and Jurgensen took over at quarterback. He led the Eagles to a 10–4 record in 1961 with an NFL-high 32 touchdowns, still an Eagles record.

"Sonny had a great arm," Hall of Fame teammate Tommy McDonald said. "He learned a lot watching Van Brocklin."

But Jurgensen won just five of 22 starts in 1962 and 1963, throwing more interceptions (39) than touchdowns (33). After the 1963 season, the Eagles fired Skorich and traded Jurgensen to the Redskins for Snead and defensive back Claude Crabb. Jurgensen was a few months shy of his thirtieth birthday, had a 17–22–2 career record and was starting over with a new team.

"I was shocked," Jurgensen said in a 2002 interview with the Pro Football Hall of Fame's website. "It was April Fool's Day and...I didn't believe [it], but I found out it was true."

Crabb lasted only two years with the Eagles. Snead won just 28 of 80 starts in seven seasons. But Jurgensen made four Pro Bowl teams with the Redskins, led the NFL in passing yards three times and in 1983 was enshrined in the Pro Football Hall of Fame.

"It was the best thing that ever happened to me, to come to Washington," Jurgensen said.

It took a long time for the Eagles franchise to recover from trading future Hall of Famer Sonny Jurgensen to the Washington Redskins after the 1963 season.

January 19, 2002

Hugh Destroys Jim Miller

Douglas Knocks Bears' QB out of Playoff Game during Interception Return

Long before the game began, Eagles cornerbacks Bobby Taylor and Al Harris were running through some routine warm-up drills in the end zone.

"Me and Al would always go out early," Taylor remembered. "We positioned ourselves in the end zone and just did some drills on our own. We did it all the time."

When word that the Bears were planning another *Super Bowl Shuffle* video reached Philadelphia just days before the Eagles-Bears 2001 playoff game, the Eagles got mad. When some Bears fans circumvented hotel security and started calling Eagles players' rooms in the middle of the night, the team got even madder. And when the Bears raised a banner before the game commemorating their 2001 NFC Central title, that was the last straw.

So when a couple Bears players began interfering with Harris and Taylor's end zone warm-up drill, Taylor was in no mood for it.

"Here comes Marty Booker and the quarterback, [Jim] Miller," Taylor said. "They start throwing fade routes at us. I was like, 'What's going on here?' Then I turned it into a one-on-one drill. They just looked at us, and I think they got punked. I said some stuff to them and they left."

Kickoff was still an hour away, but the Eagles had made a statement. They weren't going to be bullied. "That was the first time I've ever seen a football team that was truly intimidated by another football team," Hugh Douglas said. "Because we let them know, 'We cannot wait until this game gets started because we're going to whoop your ass just because you disrespected us.'"

The Bears had won 13 regular-season games, they owned the NFL's top-ranked defense, and they were virtually unbeatable at home. They were good, and wanted everybody to know it.

"We were in their house, everybody was talking about how great their defense was, and we felt like we were an afterthought," All-Pro safety Brian Dawkins said. "We went in there with a huge chip on our shoulders. We were going to do whatever we had to do to win that game."

Jim Miller (15) is crumpled by Hugh Douglas in the first half of the NFC divisional playoff on January 19, 2002, in Chicago. Miller left the game with a separated right shoulder.

The Fog Bowl

Mike Quick played in one playoff game in his career and nobody saw it—including Quick. Thirteen years before Hugh Douglas blasted Jim Miller into a figurative fog in an Eagles-Bears playoff game at Soldier Field, those teams spent an entire half playing in a very real fog.

"It was the strangest game ever," Quick said of the Fog Bowl, the 1988 Eagles-Bears playoff game. "You really couldn't see anything."

Thanks to a mass of warm air drifting off Lake Michigan mixing with cool air over Chicago, a dense fog descended on Soldier Field as the first half ended.

"We didn't think much of it at first," Quick said. "But it never stopped."

The Bears led 17–9 after the sunny first half, when the Eagles squandered several golden scoring chances.

Each team managed only a field goal in the second half, and the Eagles, in their first playoff game in seven years, lost 20–12.

"I could hardly see across the field," Eagles coach Buddy Ryan said. "They'd run a play, and I didn't know who had the ball or what the hell was going on."

The Fog Bowl was the first of three straight playoff losses that cost Ryan his job and Quick his only chance at a postseason victory.

"During my entire career, that was the one legitimate opportunity I had to go to the Super Bowl," Quick said. "And to this day I believe the main reason we didn't go was because of the fog. I really believe that was our year."

Stadium lights barely shine through the impossibly thick daytime fog at the Eagles and Bears semifinal NFC playoff game in Chicago on December 31, 1988.

The Eagles had won only one road playoff game in the previous 52 years, but they weren't leaving Chicago with a loss.

"We were going to kick their ass," Douglas said. "That was it. That was the only thing on our mind. That was a game we took very, very personally, because they basically had made their reservations to go to St. Louis [for the NFC Championship Game] and win the whole thing."

The Eagles led 6–0 early in the second quarter when Miller, looking for receiver Dez White, was intercepted by Eagles safety Damon Moore at the 2-yard line. As Moore began his return up the left sideline, Douglas found himself face to face with Miller at the 20.

"I told him, 'Don't move,'" Douglas says now. "He moved. The rest is history."

As soon as Miller headed in Moore's direction to try and tackle him, Douglas unleashed all his force into Miller, who collapsed in a heap as Moore sped by.

"On an interception, everybody's fair game," Dawkins said. "He put him down, and he put him out."

No flag was thrown, but Douglas had busted up Miller's shoulder, and the veteran quarterback was done for the day. So were the Bears. The Eagles waltzed to a 33–19 win, advancing to their first NFC Championship Game in 21 years, against Kurt Warner and the Rams in St. Louis.

"I played for the Bears the next year, and [center] Olin Kreutz would always say, 'That was a cheap shot,'" Moore said. "But I told him, 'That's football. You're going to pay a guy $190 million to throw a ball around, that guy's fair game when he's trying to make a tackle.'"

The Bears didn't have another winning season for four years. And Miller? He was never the same. He played one more season, won two games, then retired.

"As a defensive player, we're told, when somebody gets an interception, everybody make sure the quarterback's blocked, because he's probably going to be the last line of defense," Douglas said. "I guess he thought it was funny or cute that he's going to make the play, but he had on the wrong color jersey. So when he moved, he had to pay. That's the bottom line. That's how we approached the game. He had to pay."

Douglas had to pay, too. Even though he wasn't cited for a penalty, he was fined $35,000 for the hit.

"The backup quarterback [Shane Matthews] started crying about the play and that's when they fined me," Douglas said. "But it was worth it, every dime. And if I could do it again and I knew I'd be getting fined? I would do it again. I wouldn't change a thing."

Game Details

Philadelphia Eagles 33 • Chicago Bears 19

Eagles	6	7	7	13	**33**
Bears	0	7	7	5	**19**

Date: January 19, 2002
Team Records: Philadelphia 11–5, Chicago 13–3
Scoring Plays:

PHI—Akers 34-yard FG
PHI—Akers 23-yard FG
CHI—Merritt 47-yard run (Edinger PAT)
PHI—Martin 13-yard pass from McNabb (Akers PAT)
CHI—Azumah 39-yard interception return (Edinger PAT)
PHI—Staley 6-yard pass from McNabb (Akers PAT)
CHI—Edinger 38-yard FG
PHI—Akers 40-yard FG
PHI—Akers 46-yard FG
PHI—McNabb 5-yard run (Akers PAT)
CHI—Safety, Landeta ran out of end zone

They all thought Hugh was crazy even before the game. Those guys were asking me about him. Yeah, he is crazy.

—EAGLES SAFETY BRIAN DAWKINS

30

November 22, 1992

Vai Spars with the Goal Post

Sikahema Punches Out Giants Stadium Goalpost After Record-Setting Punt Return

It was a gesture packed with symbolism. Even if the guy who made the gesture didn't realize it yet.

"I had no idea what I was getting into, what it was going to mean to the city of Philadelphia," Vai Sikahema said.

Sikahema, in his first year with the Eagles after a Pro-Bowl career with the Cardinals, had just set a team record with an 87-yard return of a Sean Landeta punt for a touchdown against the Giants, giving the Eagles a 40–20 lead on their way to a 47–34 win.

The usually mild-mannered return specialist tossed the ball to the official and then turned pugilist, using a flurry of left jabs and right uppercuts on the unsuspecting Giants Stadium goal post. The sight of Sikahema turning *Rocky* at the Meadowlands made him a hero in Philadelphia, where he is now one of the top TV sports anchors.

"If I was really smart, I would have known how much that meant to the city," Sikahema said. "How much that resonated throughout Philadelphia. I didn't know. I really didn't know. I hadn't been in Philadelphia that long. I didn't even know how big the rivalry with the Giants was. I wasn't even that big on *Rocky*.

"When I tossed the ball down, I just went to the goal post and started punching it. I knew my Dad [Loni] was at his home in Phoenix watching, because the game was the national television game. It was for him.

"It was late in my career at that point. I didn't know if I'd get another [touchdown], so that was for him. It was in homage to my father."

Sikahema and his family came to the United States from Tonga so a young Vai could train under his father's guidance to be a boxer.

"That was his dream," Sikahema said. "The plan was for me to be in the 1980 Olympics. As it turned out, I was playing college football by then, and the dream turned out to be one of making the NFL instead."

Sikahema made the NFL, starred for the Cardinals, played a year in Green Bay, and then came to the Eagles as a free agent in 1992.

In a charity boxing match in Atlantic City in 2008, Sikahema KO'd former major-league slugger Jose Canseco (seven inches taller and 30 pounds heavier) in a charity boxing match in Atlantic City. That added to a legend that began 16 years earlier.

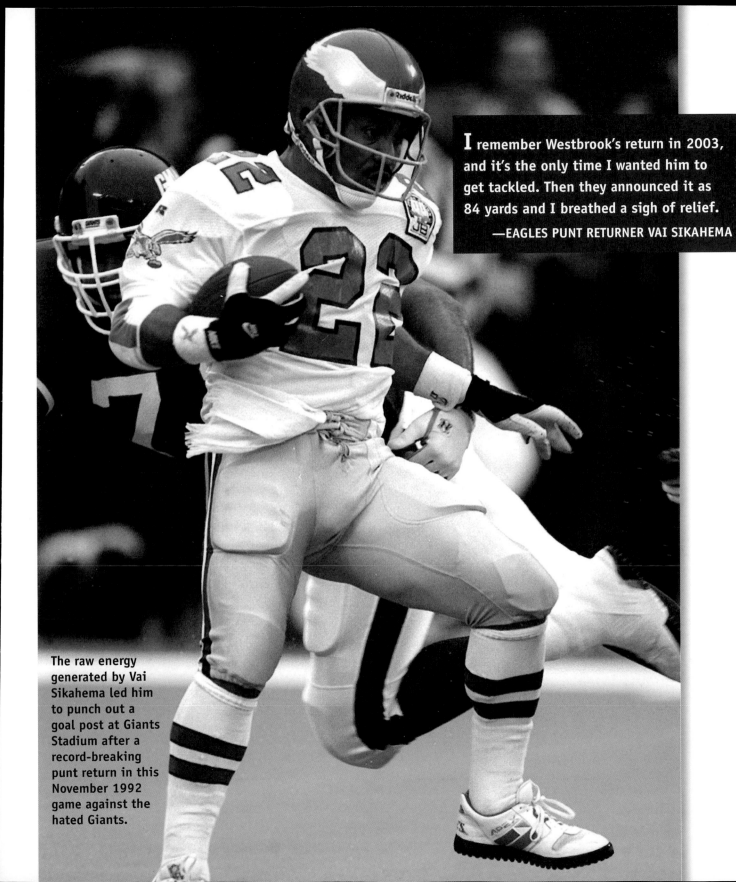

I remember Westbrook's return in 2003, and it's the only time I wanted him to get tackled. Then they announced it as 84 yards and I breathed a sigh of relief.

—EAGLES PUNT RETURNER VAI SIKAHEMA

The raw energy generated by Vai Sikahema led him to punch out a goal post at Giants Stadium after a record-breaking punt return in this November 1992 game against the hated Giants.

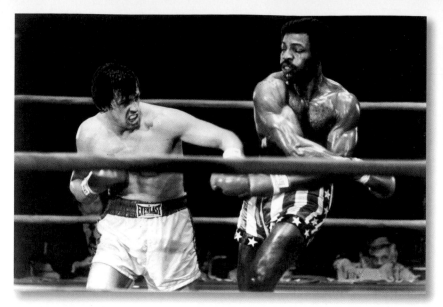

Celebrating a touchdown, Eagles punt returner Vai Sikahema unwittingly likened himself to another Philadelphia sports hero, fictional boxer Rocky Balboa (left).

Game Details

Philadelphia Eagles 47 • New York Giants 34

Eagles	0	20	20	7	**47**
Giants	10	10	7	7	**34**

Date: November 22, 1992

Team Records: Philadelphia 6–4, New York 5–5

Scoring Plays:

NYG—Bahr 35-yard FG

NYG—Meggett 14-yard pass from Hostetler (Bahr PAT)

PHI—Walker 21-yard pass from Cunningham (kick failed)

NYG—Meggett 92-yard kickoff ret (Bahr PAT)

NYG—Bahr 44-yard FG

PHI—Joyner 43-yard interception return (Ruzek PAT)

PHI—Walker 11-yard run (Ruzek PAT)

PHI—Byars 38-yard pass from Cunningham (Ruzek PAT)

PHI—Rose 3-yard punt return (Ruzek PAT)

PHI—Sikahema 87-yard punt return (kick failed)

NYG—McCaffrey 18-yard pass from Graham (Bahr PAT)

PHI—Sherman 30-yard run (Ruzek PAT)

NYG—Hampton 2-yard run (Bahr PAT)

"It's always tough to field punts there because of the wind," Sikahema said. "Landeta hung one really high and really far. It was over 60 yards. When I went back and got it, there wasn't anyone within 15 yards of me. Whenever I had room like that, I would just go straight up field and allow my wall to form.

"That's what I did. I went about 10 yards, and there was the wall. I made a hard cut to the right, and the only person I had to beat was Sean. I cut back on him. He planted his foot and blew out his knee on the play. Then William Frizzell escorted me into the end zone."

Landeta, who suffered a torn anterior cruciate ligament, became an Eagle seven years later, following two Pro Bowls and two Super Bowl titles with the Giants.

"Considering it was a cold, rainy day, it wasn't a bad punt at all," Landeta said. "He was just a terrific punt returner."

That win helped Sikahema make the playoffs for the first and only time in his eight-year career.

"I don't think Sean is mad at me anymore," Sikahema said. "We always had a great rivalry, going all the way back to when I was with the Cardinals, playing the Giants twice a year. I got him a few times, with a 50-yarder, a 60-yarder, and a couple of 40-yarders. But I used to tell him he's going to Super Bowls, and I can't even make the playoffs."

Timmy Brown

The 1966 season wasn't a pleasant one for Timmy Brown. His 3.4-yard rushing average was two yards below his NFL-leading 5.4 mark of a year earlier. He dropped off from 50 catches the previous season to 33. He ran for only three touchdowns. And he was constantly at odds with head coach Joe Kuharich.

But for one day, that was all forgotten. That was the day Brown became the first player in NFL history to return two kickoffs for touchdowns in a single game.

"I got lucky," Brown said.

Not quite. With the Eagles trailing the Cowboys 7–0 in the first quarter at Franklin Field, Brown fielded a Danny Villanueva kickoff, cut back to elude Mike Johnson, ran past Warren Livingston, then raced down the home sideline for a 93-yard touchdown. With the Cowboys ahead 17–7 in the second quarter, Brown fielded another Villanueva kickoff, broke free of Mike Connelly, eluded Livingston again, and dashed down the visiting sideline for a 90-yard kick return. The Eagles came back to win 24–23 despite just 80 yards of offense.

Brown remained the only NFL player with two kick returns of at least 90 yards for touchdowns in the same game until 1994.

When Brown demanded to be traded after the 1967 season, the Eagles shipped him to the Colts for cornerback Alvin Haymond. When Brown retired, he ranked sixth in NFL history with 235 receptions. His 62 TDs still rank fifth in Eagles history, and his five kick returns for touchdowns are sixth-most in league history.

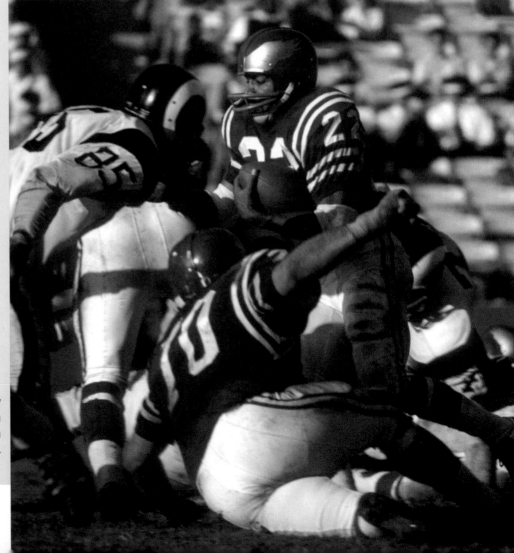

Eagles running back Timmy Brown (No. 22) rushes with the ball against the Rams on November 12, 1967.

29

December 2, 1991

The House of Pain

Hopkins Breaks Givins' Nose, Eagles Punish Oilers in "House of Pain Game"

Wes Hopkins is still waiting to meet Dan Dierdorf. On a Monday night when the Eagles punished the Houston Oilers and Hopkins put a particularly unforgettable hit on Houston wide receiver Ernest Givins, Dierdorf, an ABC broadcaster at the time, crossed the line.

"You might think I'm crazy, but of all of the things that happened that night, what I remember most is that Dan Dierdorf called me a dirty player," Hopkins recalls more than 17 years later. "It was a clean hit. I had never been called a dirty player before or after that—so I'll never forget what he said. I always wanted to talk to him about that, but to this day we've never met."

Givins wishes he never met Hopkins. Early in a game the Eagles would win 13–6 thanks to a ferocious defensive performance, Givins ran one of the crossing patterns that had become a staple of the Oilers' run-and-shoot offense. Hopkins, playing in a deep zone defense, diagnosed the play perfectly and made a hit that separated Givins from the ball and nearly separated his nose from his face.

"Wes really had him sized up to hit him, going in with his shoulder," said linebacker Seth Joyner, who had a huge game that night with eight tackles, two sacks, two forced fumbles, and two fumble recoveries. "But at the last moment, Ernest moved, and Wes reacted with a quick forearm and got him right between his facemask and his nose.

"That hit changed the whole complexion of the game. Their passing game incorporated a lot of crossing routes in the middle of the field. But after that hit, none of their guys wanted to run in the middle of the field."

The Eagles defense, under coordinator Bud Carson, came in prepared for Houston's No. 1-ranked passing attack, led by future Hall of Famer Warren Moon.

"We had a great game plan that night," Hopkins said. "They had that run-and-shoot offense, and the inside receiver would always raise his arm or his hand to let Moon know they were coming across the middle.

"Bud told me and Andre [Waters] to play a two-deep zone but to watch the receiver's hand, wait for him to come inside, then just go after him. We did it all night. We had a little inside knowledge there.

"On that play with Givins, I was actually going for the interception. Moon was staring him down on the play, and I went for it. But he had such a strong arm, the ball got there just before I did. I leaned into him with my shoulder and he ducked down, so I hit him across his face and broke his nose."

Houston's high-powered offense managed just 247 total yards that night. The Eagles defense forced five turnovers and sacked Moon four times.

The Oilers called the Astrodome "the House of Pain." After the game, in the Eagles' locker room, defensive tackle Jerome Brown barked out, "They brought the house. We brought the pain."

It all started with Hopkins' hit.

"He just plastered him," defensive tackle Andy Harmon said. "He bloodied his nose and just messed him up. He hit him so hard I think everybody in the stadium could hear it."

It was that kind of a night for an Eagles defense that helped rank the 1991 Eagles No. 1 in every major category.

"They were supposed to be the most physical team in the league, but we thought we were a pretty physical team,

Game Details

Philadelphia Eagles 13 • Houston Oilers 6

Eagles	0	0	10	3	**13**
Oilers	0	3	3	0	**6**

Date: December 2, 1991
Team Records: Philadelphia 7–5, Houston 9–3
Scoring Plays:
HOU—Del Greco 42-yard FG
PHI—Ruzek 23-yard FG
PHI—Jackson 21-yard pass from Kemp (Ruzek PAT)
HOU—Del Greco 47-yard FG
PHI—Ruzek 29-yard FG

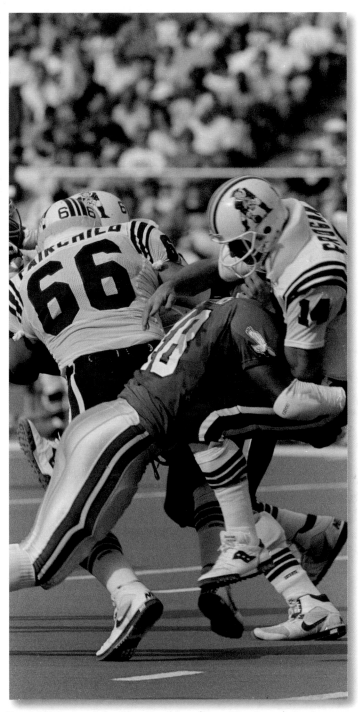

Hard-hitting safety Wes Hopkins (No. 48, above) broke Houston Oilers receiver Ernest Givins' nose in the "House of Pain Game" in December 1991.

too," cornerback Eric Allen said. "We went down there and our game plan was just to smother them. I remember Jerome [Brown] saying, 'They think they're the most physical team in the league. We're going to go show them what physical is.'

"Wes would just intimidate people. He was such a smart player and also a devastating hitter. So Warren Moon [came] across the middle and Wes just [made] a beeline toward Givins. Wes wasn't a big wrap-up guy. He was just going to come in and hit you, and you were going to go down. Now, usually, when a guy knows he's about to get hit like that, he'll turn his body so the guy hits him in the back. Givins just caught the ball and Wes just laid him out."

Andre, Jerome, and Reggie

There's a photograph from Seth Joyner's Eagles days that hangs on his office wall, a photo he looks at every day. There's Joyner with Eagles teammates Clyde Simmons, Reggie White, Jerome Brown, Eric Allen, and Andre Waters—all fixtures on the dominating Eagles defense of the late 1980s and early 1990s.

White, Brown, and Waters are gone.

"To look at that photo and know that three of those six guys are no longer with us, it's just mind-blowing," Joyner said. "It's a constant reminder of just how fragile life is."

Brown, the huge defensive tackle who always kept things light in the Eagles locker room, was 27 and in the prime of a Pro Bowl career when he was killed in a car crash on June 25, 1992. White, a first-ballot Hall of Famer, had turned 43 a week before he died from a sleep disorder on December 26, 2004. Waters, the overachieving safety who became an immediate fan favorite as an undrafted free agent, was 44 when took his own life on November 20, 2006.

"I think about those guys all the time," Wes Hopkins said. "There can't be another team in the league to lose three guys that young."

Anybody who was around them will never forget them.

"It's really unbelievable," defensive tackle Andy Harmon said. "You think about how much more they could have done with their lives. They were all such great athletes and had such great personalities. Andre was hilarious. He used to come up behind me and drill me really hard in the back and then just laugh about it. I roomed with Jerome on the road and got to know him so well. What a great guy, always laughing. And Reggie was just Reggie."

The Eagles retired White's No. 92 and Brown's No. 99 immediately upon their deaths. Waters' No. 20 was worn for 13 years by Brian Dawkins, who spoke often of his admiration for Waters and the ferocious way he played the game.

"I learned so much from all of those guys," Joyner said. "Having the opportunity to play next to Reggie for seven of my 13 years, I did a lot of growing up around him. Andre, here's a guy who nobody gave an opportunity to, and look at the career he made for himself. A very tough-minded individual committed to getting himself ready every week. Everybody on our defense wanted to make plays like Reggie and knock people out of their uniform like Andre.

"But for me, the one that hurt the most was Jerome. He was younger than me, and he was like my brother. In a blink, he's gone. It was really difficult not having him around. I was always really serious, but Jerome taught me how to keep things fun. They're all sorely missed. I think about them all the time."

28

December 15, 2003

Buck Goes Airborne

Correll Buckhalter had nowhere to go but out of bounds. It turned out to be a wise choice.

The Eagles and Dolphins were tied at 24 in a Monday night game in Miami in December 2003, but the Eagles were threatening. On first-and-goal from the 2, Donovan McNabb threw to Buckhalter on a one-lineman screen. Buckhalter caught the ball behind the line of scrimmage near the right sideline but found his route to the end zone blocked.

"Zach Thomas and Junior Seau had me penned in," Buckhalter recalls now. "[Center] Hank Fraley was blocking Seau, but I was thinking, *I have no shot to beat both these guys.* The only chance I had was to jump."

Gripping the ball in his right hand, Buckhalter flew upside down toward the sideline, the ball pointing straight down, a foot above the pylon. Buckhalter was initially ruled out at the 1-yard line, but the Eagles challenged, and replays showed the tip of the ball curling above the pylon.

"One of the most athletic plays I've ever seen," said offensive lineman Artis Hicks, who made his first NFL start in that game. "To be completely upside down, holding the ball out, and know where the pylon was in relation to his body? That's incredible."

The touchdown gave the Eagles a 34–27 win, their ninth straight.

"You pretty much know where the end zone is going to be, even if you can't really see it," Buckhalter said. "I don't think about what I'm doing, I just do it. It's all instinct."

Eagles running back Correll Buckhalter of the Philadelphia Eagles sails into the end zone for a touchdown during the game against the Miami Dolphins on December 15, 2003 at Pro Player Stadium in Miami, Florida.

Keith Byars scores the final touchdown against the Cowboys on October 25, 1987.

27

October 25, 1987

Sweet Revenge

Buddy Calls for Fake Kneel-Down in 1987 Rematch with Hated Cowboys

It began in the final minutes of a Cowboys blowout in Dallas. It ended two weeks later in the final minute of an Eagles blowout in Philly, with a play you've never seen before and likely will never see again.

The week after the month-long 1987 NFL players' strike ended, the Eagles hosted the Dallas Cowboys and led their NFC East rival, 30–20, late in the fourth quarter. The Eagles' defense held, the offense got the ball back and the Cowboys were out of timeouts. Three snaps and three kneel-downs would secure the win for Buddy Ryan's team.

The game was over. The Eagles just had to run out the clock to win. But a win wasn't enough for Ryan. Not two weeks after, revered Cowboys head coach Tom Landry had used seven of his regular players—including three All-Pros—against Ryan's ragtag bunch of replacement players.

"Buddy's pregame talks were never long," linebacker Garry Cobb said. "He always got right to the point. Before that game, he let us know that the Cowboys disrespected us and we couldn't allow that. Of course, he dropped a few F-bombs in there, too. But we knew he wanted this one more than ever."

On first down, quarterback Randall Cunningham took the snap, took a knee, and the clock continued to run down on what would be a sweet Eagles victory.

Second down followed the same script. Snap, kneel-down.

"We were in kneel-down mode, what we called victory," wide receiver Mike Quick said. "We didn't see this coming."

Who could? On third down, as the seconds continued to run off the clock and the fans headed for the exits, Cunningham again took the snap, and began kneeling down. But this time he stopped, stood up, and threw deep for Quick.

Pass interference was called on Dallas cornerback Everson Walls, the Eagles got the ball at the 1-yard line, and running back Keith Byars scored a rub-it-in touchdown on the next play for a 37–20 win.

"I didn't know we were going to do that until we did it," Cunningham said. "That was Buddy being Buddy. It's the end of the game, and we're taking a knee, letting the clock run out. We're going to win.

"Then he said, 'Do it. Fake the knee and throw it deep.' So, we did it and got pass interference on the play and got

"You remember what happened in that [strike] game," Ryan said. "He put his front four back in the game, Dorsett, the quarterback White. They said I opened a can of worms. Hell, he opened the can of worms. I closed it."

Cobb, now a radio personality in Philadelphia, was with the Eagles in 1987. He joined the Cowboys the following season. "Word started to spread on the sidelines that something was going to happen," Cobb said. "I think Otho [Davis, the trainer] started it. So we were all kind of waiting to see what it was. When he did that 'kneel-down,' that was classic Buddy.

"The thing is, Buddy intimidated the Cowboys—the whole organization. They were still talking about that play the next year."

Buddy Ryan was furious when Tom Landry played his regulars during a 1987 strike game against the Eagles. He got his revenge two weeks later.

the ball at the 1-yard line. It was crazy, but that was Buddy. I knew he was mad at Dallas for what happened in the strike game, but I didn't know what he was going to do."

Ryan was still furious that Landry had used stars such as future Hall of Famers Tony Dorsett and Randy White, starting quarterback Danny White, and Pro Bowl defensive end Ed "Too Tall" Jones against Ryan's strike team in the Cowboys' 41–22 win two weeks earlier.

Game Details

Philadelphia Eagles 37 • Dallas Cowboys 20

Eagles	3	10	7	17	**37**
Cowboys	3	7	3	7	**20**

Date: October 25, 1987

Team Records: Philadelphia 1–4, Dallas 3–2

Scoring Plays:

DAL—Ruzek 23-yard FG

PHI—McFadden 46-yard FG

PHI—McFadden 45-yard FG

PHI—Spagnola 10-yard pass from Cunningham (McFadden PAT)

DAL—Walker 1-yard run (Ruzek PAT)

DAL—Ruzek 25-yard FG

PHI—Toney 1-yard run (McFadden PAT)

PHI—McFadden 21-yard FG

PHI—Spagnola 5-yard pass from Cunningham (McFadden PAT)

DAL—Dorsett 19-yard pass from White (Ruzek PAT)

PHI—Byars 1-yard run (McFadden PAT)

Buddy and Aikman

The road to the Hall of Fame was not an easy one for Troy Aikman, and Buddy Ryan is one of the biggest reasons why.

Aikman arrived in the NFL in 1989, just in time to incur the wrath of Ryan's ferocious defense at the height of its potency. Ryan became Eagles head coach in 1986, and from 1988 through 1990 the Eagles reached the playoffs thanks in large part to a vicious pass rush that reduced even the best quarterbacks in the league to rubble.

Aikman was so overmatched in those early games, it's a wonder he survived. He had little talent around him, the Eagles' defense was stocked with All-Pros, and Ryan attacked him savagely. Aikman lost his first six starts against the Eagles, throwing three touchdowns and 10 interceptions and putting up just 40 points, about 6.5 per game.

"I still have nightmares about playing the Eagles," Aikman says now.

Although Aikman eventually turned the tables on the Eagles, going 13–3 in his next 16 starts against the Birds and knocking them out of the playoffs en route to winning two of his three Super Bowls, those early meetings left quite an impression on Aikman, mentally and physically.

"The first time I played them, it was my rookie year, and that was the Bounty Bowl, when Buddy put a bounty on our kicker, Luis Zendejas, who had started the year with the Eagles," Aikman said. "I'm not kidding you, after that game, I had X-rays on both knees, both shoulders, and my elbow. I really thought they were going to put me in a body cast. I've never been beaten up so bad in my life.

> **B**uddy hated the Cowboys and especially Tom Landry. And Tom never understood Buddy.
>
> **—LINEBACKER GARRY COBB**

"I remember thinking, *I never want to play this team again*. Then somebody told me, 'You know, we have to go to Philadelphia and play these guys again in two weeks,' and I said, 'You've got to be kidding me. As bad as they punished me?'"

The rematch was at Veterans Stadium, and the Eagles won that one, too.

"They were pelting us with snowballs from the time we got there 'til the time we left," Aikman said. "I never took my helmet off the whole day."

Ryan was fired after the 1990 season, but he and Aikman crossed paths again in the summer of 1993, when Ryan was the Oilers' defensive coordinator.

"I was coming off back surgery and we had a scrimmage against Houston," Aikman said. "I wasn't practicing, so I had a chance to visit with Buddy, who I'd never really talked to very much, and I enjoyed getting to know him a little bit. As it turned out, our last preseason game was against the Oilers at the Alamodome, and I hadn't practiced very much, but I was going to play a couple series. So before the game, I said to him, 'Hey, let's take it easy on me. I'm coming off back surgery.' And he said, 'If you line up over center, you will get hit.' I'll never forget it. That was Buddy."

26

November 10, 1991

The Comeback

Fifteen seconds into the second quarter, the Eagles trailed the Cleveland Browns by 23 points.

"We just weren't ready," wide receiver Calvin Williams said. "I think we underestimated the Browns, and we definitely underestimated the atmosphere there. That Dawg Pound was crazy. I remember us getting beer poured on us right from the start."

Those rowdy Cleveland fans quieted down when Williams caught a five-yard touchdown pass from Jim McMahon late in the fourth quarter to give the Eagles a 32–30 win in November 1991.

"We kept coming back and coming back," Williams said. "I knew we were going to win when [Webster Slaughter] tried to catch that punt at the 2-yard line. That was the turning point."

Slaughter, a Pro Bowl receiver, made the mistake of trying to field Jeff Feagles' punt in the shadow of his end zone and compounded the error by allowing Eagles linebacker Britt Hager to strip the ball from him. The Eagles recovered at the 5-yard line, setting up McMahon's game-winner to Williams.

"Jim was looking at me and I was looking at him," Williams said. "When you have your quarterback's eyes like that, you know you're getting the ball."

Despite a severe elbow injury, McMahon passed for 341 yards and three touchdowns, his second-best passing day ever.

"We're down something like 30 to negative 10, their crowd is in the game—it makes you want to come back so bad," Eagles receiver Fred Barnett said. "You just want to shut everybody up and send them home."

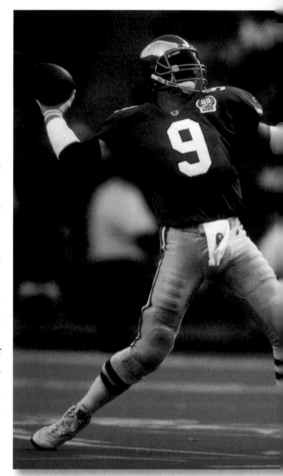

Jim McMahon launches a deep ball during his brief stint with the Eagles. His touchdown pass to Calvin Williams in a November 1991 game against the Browns capped a 341-yard, three-touchdown day for the veteran quarterback.

25

December 6, 1992

Seth's Miracle

Joyner's One-Handed Interception of Salisbury and TD Return Turn Around Season

It was a play not many linebackers could make. Heck, it was a play not many cornerbacks could make. And Seth Joyner was only able to make it because he was out of position.

The Eagles had seen a 21–10 lead over the Vikings turn into 21–17 lead, and now the Vikings had the ball again. The Eagles couldn't afford to blow this game. They had already lost five of their last eight, and a scintillating 4–0 start had turned into a disappointing 7–5 record with a month left. The Vikings were 9–3 and boasted the NFL's fourth-ranked offense, and now they were roaring back, one drive away from most likely dashing the Eagles' playoff hopes.

They began with four and a half minutes left on their 30-yard line. On first-and-10, quarterback Sean Salisbury chose a safe, short swing pass to Pro Bowl tailback Terry Allen. He threw toward Allen, who was waiting in the flat near the left sideline.

"I completely read it wrong," Joyner said. "All game long, I'd been blitzing and keeping Terry Allen in the backfield. I'd run him over and get to the quarterback. I was just locked in on rushing the quarterback, but on that particular play, I'm on my way to the quarterback and all of a sudden I see Terry out on a swing route out of the corner

of my eye—and I'm supposed to be covering him. *Oh crap.* I got caught in no-man's land, in between Salisbury and Terry."

Salisbury made the correct read and threw behind Joyner, toward Allen. But Joyner reached behind him, caught the ball one-handed, left-handed, and virtually behind his back. He ran 24 yards for a touchdown, and just like that, the Eagles led 28–17.

The game was over.

"I knew I was in a bad position," Joyner says today. "I just kind of stuck my hand behind me and it hit my hand and stayed there. I'm right-handed, but when I was a kid, I taught myself how to hit a baseball left-handed and shoot basketball left-handed. I always had a ball in my hand, and all the offensive coaches would say, 'Hey, you're a defensive player, put that ball down.' None of the coaches were complaining that day."

That win woke up the Eagles, who had won just three games in the previous two months. They didn't lose again in the regular season, finishing 11–5 and reaching the playoffs for the only time under head coach Rich Kotite. They traveled to New Orleans for a wild-card game and recorded the franchise's first road playoff win in 43 years and first postseason win in 12 years.

And if Joyner hadn't made that play? Who knows.

"Football is such a game of reactions. I didn't have any thought process, I just reacted," he said.

Joyner is the only player in NFL history with at least 20 interceptions and 50 sacks. He scored five touchdowns, four of them in 1991 and 1992. He made a ton of big plays, but that one was the biggest.

"I thought he was too far upfield to get it," Salisbury told reporters after the game. "If I throw it another six inches higher, maybe he doesn't. It was that close. But then, throwing it higher leaves the receiver hanging out to dry. He may or may not dress in a phone booth. There are not many people in the NFL that could make that play."

Talk about your great linebackers. Junior Seau? Not even close. Seth could do everything.
—EAGLES CORNERBACK ERIC ALLEN

Game Details

Philadelphia Eagles 28 • Minnesota Vikings 17

Eagles	7	7	7	7	**28**
Vikings	3	7	0	7	**17**

Date: December 6, 1992

Team Records: Philadelphia 7–5, Minnesota 9–3

Scoring Plays:

MIN—Reveiz 32-yard FG

PHI—Cunningham 1-yard run (Ruzek PAT)

MIN—Allen 3-yard run (Reveiz PAT)

PHI—Sherman 1-yard run (Ruzek PAT)

PHI—Cunningham 1-yard run (Ruzek PAT)

MIN—Allen 1-yard run (Reveiz PAT)

PHI—Joyner 24-yard interception return (Ruzek PAT)

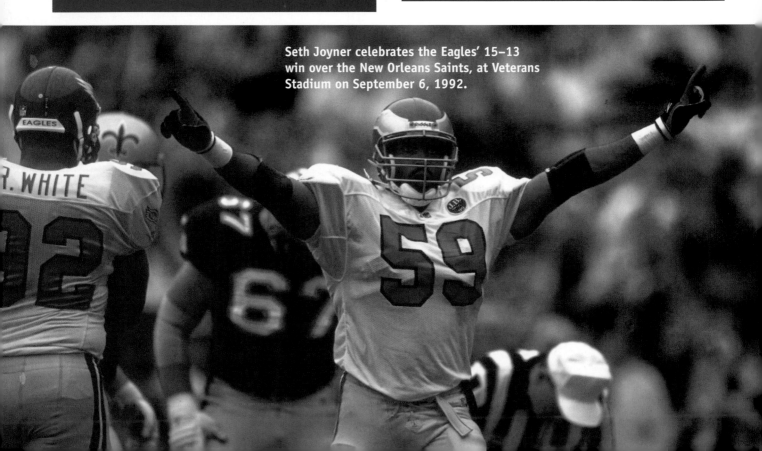

Seth Joyner celebrates the Eagles' 15–13 win over the New Orleans Saints, at Veterans Stadium on September 6, 1992.

Seth Joyner

When head coach Buddy Ryan released Seth Joyner after his rookie training camp, he told him to stay in touch, maybe a roster spot would open up.

"After the first two games, I drove down to Philly and told Buddy, 'I'm sitting around going crazy, are you going to bring me back?'" Joyner said. "He let me drive all the way back home [to Spring Valley, N.Y.], and when I got there, he had already left a message with my mom, telling me to be at practice the next day."

Joyner made the most of his second chance. He piled up 52 sacks, 24 interceptions, and 26 forced fumbles in 13 NFL seasons, the first eight with the Eagles.

"My career was all about proving people wrong," Joyner said. "I played with a lot of anger and animosity because a lot of people didn't believe in me. I wanted to show everybody what a mistake they made.

"If I had 100-plus sacks, I'd probably get some Hall of Fame consideration. But I'd rather be known as a linebacker who could do it all."

Nobody else in NFL history recorded 50 sacks and 20 interceptions. Joyner stands alone.

"Seth had a great feel for the game like a middle linebacker but was very athletic, like an outside linebacker, and had the ability to rush the passer, like a defensive end," teammate Eric Allen said. "And then to have those great football instincts and be able to make plays on the ball? He was flat-out nasty on the football field."

Seth Joyner's spectacular interception in a 1992 game against the Vikings was one of the most memorable in a career of big plays from the high-motor linebacker.

24

January 4, 2009

Westbrook for 71 Yards

Their offense was nonexistent. The Eagles clung to a two-point lead, thanks mainly to their defense. The Vikings had shut down Brian Westbrook all day and were growing more and more confident. And then Westbrook, though reduced by injuries to a shadow of his former self, turned a six-yard screen pass into an electrifying 71-yard fourth-quarter touchdown, and the Eagles went on to win 26–14 in their 2008 wild-card game at the Metrodome.

"If you keep giving him the ball, eventually he's going to make a play," cornerback Joselio Hanson said. "It's just a matter of time."

Once he caught Donovan McNabb's pass—which just missed right guard Nick Cole's helmet—Westbrook hesitated for a split second to set up the play.

"He has an unbelievable ability to just stop and freeze a defense," head coach Andy Reid said. "Once they stop—because they don't know which way he's going—he has the advantage."

As Westbrook weaved in and out of traffic, Cole obliterated cornerback Antoine Winfield, center Jamaal Jackson blasted safety Tyrell Johnson, and fullback Correll Buckhalter took care of linebacker Ben Leber.

Down the field, wideout Kevin Curtis dashed from across the field to knock cornerback Cedric Griffin out of the way, and rookie DeSean Jackson sprinted 40 yards to get in front of cornerback Benny Sapp and block him legally as Westbrook collapsed into the end zone.

"We needed some momentum," he said. "That touchdown provided that momentum. No matter how many times a team stops me, I still continue trying to make those plays."

Brian Westbrook squirts out of the attempted tackle of Vikings cornerback Antoine Winfield on a 71-yard touchdown reception in t[he] fourth quarter of a playoff game [in] Minneapolis on January 4, 2009. The Eagles won, 26–14.

23

September 17, 1989

"Give Me the Ball, Big Al"

Harris Recovery, Hopkins Return Cap Rally from 20-Point Deficit vs. Redskins

The Eagles had already overcome a 20-point deficit. Now they needed a defensive stand to get the ball back and give quarterback Randall Cunningham one last chance. Then Washington running back Gerald Riggs broke free up the right sideline for a career-long 58-yard run. So much for another comeback. Until Redskins coach Joe Gibbs gave Riggs the ball on the next play, too.

"He had to be tired after that 58-yard run," Eagles cornerback Eric Allen said.

And when linebacker Seth Joyner tackled Riggs, he pushed him into center Raleigh McKenzie, and the ball came loose. After piling up a Redskins franchise-record 221 yards, it was Riggs who had given the Eagles life.

"I remember it's near the end of the game, and I'm telling the guys, I especially remember telling Clyde [Simmons]... 'You got to believe, you got to believe. We can still win this game,'" linebacker Al Harris said. "I really was thinking we could still win this game, but then Riggs broke that long run. When that ball popped out, it was a miracle."

Harris recovered Riggs' fumble at the Eagles 31-yard line and handed the ball to safety Wes Hopkins, who returned it to the Washington 4. On the next play, Cunningham threw a short touchdown pass to tight end Keith Jackson, capping a career-best 447-yard game and giving the Eagles a 42–37 win.

"Riggs was a teammate of mine at Arizona State, so I knew him a little," Harris said. "But I never expected him to go for 200-plus against us. One of the things about him, though, was when he got it going and got in rhythm behind those Hogs, he was tough to stop."

Riggs and Washington's offense had their way with Buddy Ryan's famed defense that day. Until it mattered most.

"We were in the 46, because I was on the left side," Harris said. "Riggs is running down the sideline and the ball just popped out. I see it, and you're taught to jump on a loose ball, and that's what I did. I'm on the ground, and I realize nobody has touched me. Guys are yelling, 'Get up, get up.' As I get up, [Washington tackle] Jim Lachey hits me, and that's when I hear Wes yelling, 'Give it up, Big Al! Give it up.'

"Now I'm going backwards, and Wes is there and I'm trying to give him the ball. Actually, if I let it go sooner, Wes might have scored. He finally gets it, and I'm on my

Keith Jackson's four-yard touchdown catch from Randall Cunningham in the game's final moments capped a rally from a 20-point deficit and gave the Eagles a 42–37 win at RFK Stadium over the Redskins in September 1989.

It looked like Al was standing in quicksand. Wes just ran over and took the ball from him.

—EAGLES LINEBACKER SETH JOYNER

back watching as he's running downfield. I'm thinking, 'We are going to win this game.'"

Hopkins thought so, too, once he was able to get the ball from the big linebacker.

"What I remember most is that the Redskins had the game in control," Hopkins said. "And they usually were the kind of team that didn't let you back in it. Then Riggs fumbled and Al recovered. There wasn't a lot of time left, so I knew I had to do something.

"I took it from him and just tried to get as close to the end zone as I could. I almost got there, but I was running out of gas. I was going to lateral it again, but the only person I saw was Jerome [Brown], and I thought that might not be a good idea.

Game Details

Philadelphia Eagles 42 • Washington Redskins 37

Eagles	7	7	7	21	**42**
Redskins	20	10	0	7	**37**

Date: September 17, 1989

Team Records: Philadelphia 1–0, Washington 0–1

Scoring Plays:

WAS—Clark 80-yard pass from Rypien (kick failed)

WAS—Riggs 41-yard run (Lohmiller PAT)

WAS—Byner 11-yard pass from Rypien (Lohmiller PAT)

PHI—Jackson 17-yard pass from Cunningham (Zendejas PAT)

WAS—Clark 5-yard pass from Rypien (Lohmiller PAT)

PHI—Toney 3-yard run (Zendejas PAT)

WAS—Lohmiller 25-yard FG

PHI—Jackson 5-yard pass from Cunningham (Zendejas PAT)

PHI—Carter 5-yard pass from Cunningham (Zendejas PAT)

WAS—Monk 43-yard pass from Rypien (Lohmiller PAT)

PHI—Quick 2-yard pass from Cunningham (Zendejas PAT)

PHI—Jackson 4-yard pass from Cunningham (Zendejas PAT)

Randall Gets Paid

One of the craziest days in Eagles history began in the Arlington, Virginia, hotel room of team president Harry Gamble.

The morning of the Eagles' improbable come-from-behind 42–37 win over the Redskins at RFK Stadium in Washington, quarterback Randall Cunningham, his representatives, and Gamble got together to hammer out a new contract.

"I knew they had been talking," Cunningham said. "And then it just all got done that morning."

Cunningham, who a few years earlier signed a deal worth over $1 million per year, signed a five-year deal worth $15 million, which in 1989 was a ton of money.

He went out that afternoon and completed 34 of 46 passes for a then-franchise-record 447 yards and a career-high five touchdowns. In the second half alone, as the Eagles came back from 20 points down, he was 21-for-27 for 267 yards and four touchdowns.

"That was the talk all before the game," linebacker Al Harris said. "Word had started to spread about Randall's new contract. Then he went out and played the best game I had ever seen him play—the best I'd ever seen any quarterback play."

In the morning, the Eagles had made Cunningham the NFL's highest-paid quarterback. In the afternoon, he showed exactly why they did it.

Randall Cunningham was a fan favorite in Philadelphia for his spectacular play on the field.

"That was my best game," Cunningham said. "That was as good as I can play."

Was it a coincidence that on the same day the Eagles paid Cunningham like a superstar, he played like one?

"Maybe," he said, "that's why I played so good."

"But that was the way we played, as a defense. We wanted to score. It wasn't enough to just get the turnover. We wanted to score, too."

The Eagles had won only three of their previous 22 games in Washington, a stretch that dated back to the mid-1960s. But this time, nothing was going to stop them. Not even a 20-point deficit.

"I'd been around long enough to know anything can happen in a game," Ryan said. "And with the guys we had back then, you were never out of it. But that game was unusual because it was so high-scoring. Most of our games, especially against Washington, were low-scoring. We had to outscore them that day because nobody was playing any defense—until Al made that play. He saved us with that one."

Harris knew somebody would.

"I'll never forget this: after the game, Clyde comes up to me and says, 'Big Al, you were right,'" Harris said. "I just knew somehow, and don't ask me how, we were going to win that game."

22

September 3, 2000

The Onside Kick

Eagles Stun Cowboys with Season-Opening Gadget Play

When Eagles special teams coach John Harbaugh first approached special teams captain Ike Reese with the plan, Reese just stared at him. An onside kick? *To open the season?*

"He was scared it wouldn't work," Harbaugh says now. "He said, 'You're kidding me. No freaking way.'"

Harbaugh wasn't kidding. And eventually, Reese came around—sort of.

"I told him, 'If you feel we can do it, let's do it,'" Reese said. "But I was saying to myself, *These are the Cowboys. We're on the road. It's the first game of the season. What if it doesn't work?*"

The Eagles were 14–33–1 in the previous three years. They hadn't won an opener since 1996. They had won just one of their last 10 games at Texas Stadium.

"You're talking about a team that was looking for something to grab onto, some hope to grab onto," Reese says now. "A team that was tired of being kicked around, tired of being called the worst team in the league. We needed some reassurance that we were good."

As early as mid-August, second-year head coach Andy Reid had decided that if the Eagles lost the coin toss on opening day, the season would begin with an onside kick. Reid had noticed that the Cowboys' kick-return unit was vunerable to an onside kick. And he wanted to open the season with something dramatic, something to help make the Eagles relevant again.

"Prior to the game, Andy came into the huddle, and he was like, 'What do you all think of doing an onside kick?'" Reese said. "First of all, it's the opening kickoff of the season, so we're ready to go down the field and kill somebody anyway. So he asked us do we think we can recover the football, and we were all in a tizzy. 'Yeah, we will recover.'"

Propelled by an opening season onside kick, Duce Staley ran for 201 yards in the Eagles' 41–14 rout of the Cowboys in September 2000.

David Akers kicked it, Dameane Douglas recovered it, and three hours later the Eagles had stunned the favored Cowboys 41–14, matching their most lopsided win ever against their biggest rival.

"I'm on the sideline and I was so damn nervous I could barely stand up," said Harbaugh, now head coach of the Ravens. "I thought [Cowboys special teams coach] Joe Avezzano was staring at me, and I was trying to act nonchalant. When Akers kicked it, I remember thinking, *Oh crap, we're actually doing it.*"

Other than Reid, Harbaugh and the guys on the kickoff team, nobody knew what was coming.

"I'm watching Dave get ready to kick off and I'm thinking, *Boy, his approach looks funny*," said Brad Childress, then Eagles quarterbacks coach and now head coach of the Vikings. "Then it was, *Holy crap. I can't believe we're doing this.*"

Reid and Harbaugh had noticed the front line of the Cowboys' kick return unit cheated back too soon, dropping off before the ball was even kicked.

"You're taught as a return team to not take off until you see the ball kicked," Reese said. "But we knew their front line bailed out early, and that's exactly what they did."

Akers plopped the ball in the air 12 yards—two more than the required 10 yards. Reese and fellow linebackers Barry Gardner and Mike Caldwell formed a wall around the football and the sure-handed Douglas caught it on a fly at the 42-yard line.

"It worked out perfectly," Reese said. "Akers did a great job selling it, and by the time they realized what happened, it was too late and D1 [Douglas] didn't have any resistance. We actually didn't even need to block anybody because they bailed out so fast."

Nine plays later, Donovan McNabb, making his first opening-day start, threw a one-yard touchdown pass to tight end Jeff Thomason, and the rout was on. Duce Staley finished with 201 rushing yards—the most by an Eagle in 51 years—and the defense knocked Troy Aikman out of the game before the first quarter ended.

Philadelphia Eagles special teams coordinator John Harbaugh talks during a news conference after practice in August 2006. Harbaugh was hired in January 2008 as head coach of the Baltimore Ravens and led them to the playoffs in his rookie season.

"The element of surprise can have a great effect on a team," Staley said. "A lot of times, teams can't handle it. They're going out there to start the game, they've got their plays ready, they're set to march down the field. All of a sudden, we get the ball back and it takes all the air out for them. I don't think they ever recovered from those first four or five seconds of that game."

The Eagles made the playoffs, their first of seven trips to the postseason in the next nine years. And it all started with that onside kick.

"It was a statement about what kind of team we were going to be," Harbaugh said. "It said we weren't afraid, we weren't scared. It said, 'If these crazy bastards will open the season with an onside kick on the road, they'll try anything.'"

Game Details

Philadelphia Eagles 41 • Dallas Cowboys 14

Eagles	14	10	3	14	**41**
Cowboys	0	6	0	8	**14**

Date: September 3, 2000

Team Records: Philadelphia 1–0, Dallas 0–1

Scoring Plays:

PHI—Thomason 1-yard pass from McNabb (Akers PAT)

PHI—Staley 1-yard run (Akers PAT)

PHI—Trotter 27-yard interception return (Akers PAT)

PHI—Akers 33-yard FG

DAL—Seder 34-yard FG

DAL—Seder 38-yard FG

PHI—Akers 37-yard FG

PHI—McNabb 3-yard run

PHI—Mitchell 6-yard run

DAL—Galloway 4-yard pass from Cunningham (Ismail pass from Cunningham)

Pickle Juice

Hugh Douglas had heard enough.

"We're sitting in the locker room, and everybody is like, 'It's so hot, it's so hot,'" Douglas said. "I finally stood up and said, 'You know what? Yeah. It's hot. But I don't want to hear another freaking thing about how hot it is. We've got a football game to play. F–– the heat. F–– the Cowboys. F–– Dallas. Just f–– it. Let's go out and kick their ass.'"

And that's just what they did. It was 109 degrees at kickoff, the hottest game in NFL history. On the Texas Stadium turf, it was 140.

The Eagles, who had lost nine of their last 10 against Troy Aikman, Emmitt Smith, Michael Irvin, and the Cowboys, now had something else to overcome. But after downing a healthy dose of pickle juice administered by trainer Rick Burkholder, the Eagles shrugged off the brutal conditions and burned the Cowboys, 41–14, on Opening Day 2000, propelling them to their first playoff season in four years.

"In his pregame speech, Andy [Reid] said, 'Nothing you're going to go through will be as tough as what you went through in training camp,'" Ike Reese said. "And he wasn't lying. Andy had us ready to go."

And the pickle juice? Eight years later, Burkholder admits it was all a hoax.

"It has salt in it, so it doesn't hurt," Burkholder said. "But really, it was mental more than anything. If they think it's helping them, it's helping them. It gave them confidence to go out and not worry about the heat."

That might have been the first time I pulled for us to kick off.

—EAGLES HEAD COACH ANDY REID

21

December 20, 1992

"I Finally Got Gary Clark"

Allen Adjustment Foils Rypien and Redskins, Sends Eagles to Playoffs

He returned eight interceptions for touchdowns. He made a play that NFL Films founder Steve Sabol called "the greatest interception return in NFL history." He picked off 54 passes in his career, more than 11 of the 20 defensive backs enshrined in the Hall of Fame.

But ask Eric Allen what moment in his brilliant 14-year career he's most proud of, and he'll tell you about one that doesn't even exist in the box score or stat sheet. It was one in which he barely touched the football.

"That play really was my signature play because it wasn't made that Sunday," Allen said. "It was made during the week of preparation and film study and understanding what the offense was trying to do."

Allen was in his fifth NFL season in 1992, already established as a perennial Pro Bowl cornerback. The Eagles and Redskins went into their late-December showdown with a playoff berth at stake. The winner was on their

way to the postseason; the loser would be scrambling for a playoff berth on the last day of the season.

The Redskins led 13–7 in the third quarter before the Eagles took the lead on Randall Cunningham's 28-yard touchdown pass to Calvin Williams and a 23-yard Roger Ruzek field goal. With 3:35 left in the game, the Redskins took over at their own 5-yard line and, led by reigning Super Bowl MVP Mark Rypien, marched 85 yards to the Eagles' 5-yard line, where they had four shots at a game-winning touchdown.

The Eagles thwarted the Redskins' first three chances. The next play determined the winner. With two seconds showing on the clock and the Eagles leading 17–13, Allen stood ready in man coverage on four-time Pro Bowl receiver Gary Clark. The season was on the line.

"For every cornerback, there's one guy who always gives him problems, and for me that guy was Gary Clark," Allen says today.

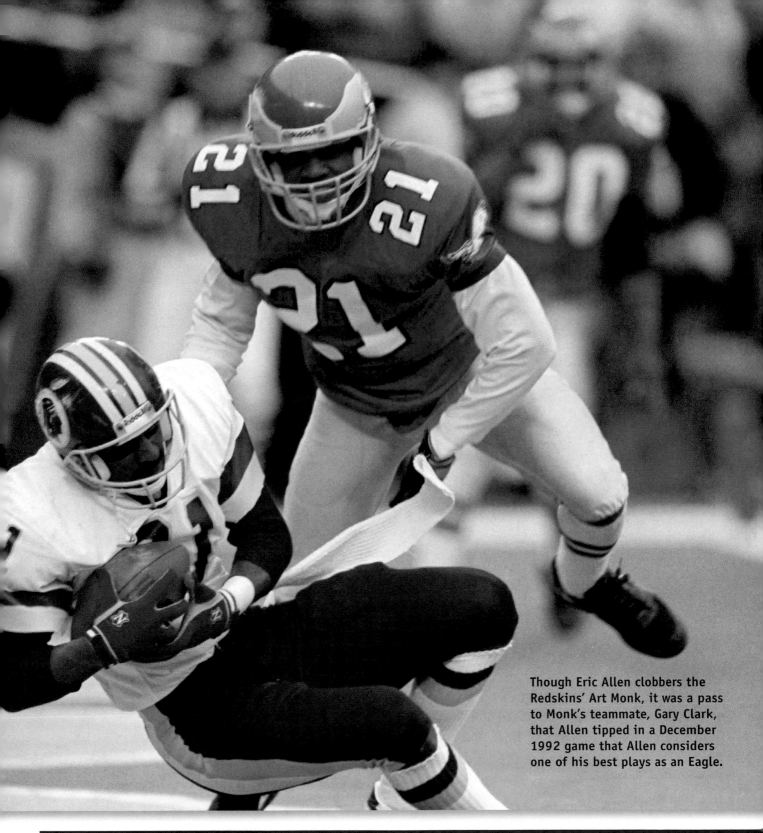

Though Eric Allen clobbers the Redskins' Art Monk, it was a pass to Monk's teammate, Gary Clark, that Allen tipped in a December 1992 game that Allen considers one of his best plays as an Eagle.

"He was a quick, competitive guy who would never give up. Some guys, if you keep pounding them long enough—maybe pick off a ball—eventually, they'll say, 'Hey, it's not my day,' and pack it in. Gary, you could knock him out, he'd get right back up."

The Redskins had other great wideouts in two-time 1,000-yard receiver Ricky Sanders and future Hall of Famer Art Monk. But Sanders was three years removed from his last 1,000-yard season, and Monk was 35 years old and beyond his prime. So as he prepared for the game's deciding play, Allen was focused primarily on his nemesis, Clark.

"The Redskins weren't a big fade team," Allen said. "So I figured they'd isolate Gary Clark, where if the defensive back played him inside, he'd run outside, and if he was played outside, he'd run inside. I was playing inside because sometimes Bud [Carson, defensive coordinator] had me blitz out of that, and I'm thinking I'll probably have to jam him. I'm going through all this stuff in my head, waiting for the play to start.

Game Details

Philadelphia Eagles 17 • Washington Redskins 13

Eagles	0	7	7	3	**17**
Redskins	0	13	0	0	**13**

Date: December 20, 1992
Team Records: Philadelphia 9–5, Washington 9–5
Scoring Plays:
WAS—Lohmiller 29-yard FG
PHI—Sherman 21-yard run (Ruzek PAT)
WAS—Sanders 62-yard pass from Rypien (Lohmiller PAT)
WAS—Lohmiller 41-yard FG
PHI—Williams 28-yard pass from Cunningham (Ruzek PAT)
PHI—Ruzek 23-yard FG

> **I** had my arms out just waiting for the ball to get to me. Then Allen reached out and knocked it down. It was a great play on his part.
>
> —REDSKINS WIDE RECEIVER GARY CLARK

"Then Rypien sends Sanders in motion, knowing I'm going to have to move with him. Now, Otis [Smith] is the outside corner, so I'm going in motion with Ricky and that's leaving Otis on Gary Clark, and that's the matchup they're looking for. They're thinking, *What can we do to get Eric Allen away from the play?* So the play starts, and I realize what's happening and I think, *I'm not going to allow it.* Otis became a great player, but he was still young and that would have been a tough matchup for him. So I leave my man wide open and go back the opposite direction, and exactly what I thought: Rypien is throwing to Clark, and he's sitting there, wide open, just waiting for the ball in the end zone. I come up and lunge and barely get my finger on the ball, and it falls incomplete and we win the game.

"Three inches more and he catches that ball. If I had waited one split second longer before I made that decision, he catches that ball. Everything worked perfectly for them on that play except I didn't go for the bait. It was such an unbelievable feeling because I just trusted my instincts. I wouldn't have gone back over to that side if I wasn't 100 percent sure what they were doing."

The game was over and the Eagles had their win and playoff berth. They went on to beat the Saints in a wild-card game, the only postseason win for Allen, Reggie White, Seth Joyner, and the rest of the famed Gang Green defense of the late 1980s and early 1990s.

"As the ball hit the ground, I started running down the field on their sideline," Allen said. "The crowd was ecstatic. They were crazy. We were in the playoffs. It was an unbelievable moment. Inside, I was thinking, *I finally got Gary Clark. I finally got my nemesis.*"

Free Agent Exodus

One by one, they left. Keith Jackson went after the 1991 season. Reggie White and Keith Byars were gone after 1992. Seth Joyner and Clyde Simmons left after 1993. Eric Allen was through by 1994.

The Great Free Agent Exodus tore the heart out of a franchise.

"Buddy [Ryan] getting fired was really the first domino to fall," Joyner said. "The pieces were in place, but then they brought in Rich Kotite as head coach, and we just knew it wasn't a situation where we could win. Once free agency came about, as players, we realized the organization wasn't truly committed to winning. Guys started leaving and things slowly fell apart."

Allen, Byars, Jackson, Joyner, Simmons, and White were named to a combined 19 Pro Bowl teams as Eagles and 11 after they left. Only Simmons failed to make a Pro Bowl with his new team, although he should have in 1995, when he had 11 sacks and forced six fumbles with the Cardinals.

"Instead of adding outstanding players, we were subtracting them," Allen said. "I would have loved to have played my whole career in Philly, but there were so many issues we dropped the ball on as a franchise. I mean, how do you let Reggie White leave? I don't care how much money he wants, the guy is the best player in the National Football League. And you just let him leave? No way anybody can say they're a better team without a Reggie White. I looked around and thought, *This just is not the team I envisioned*."

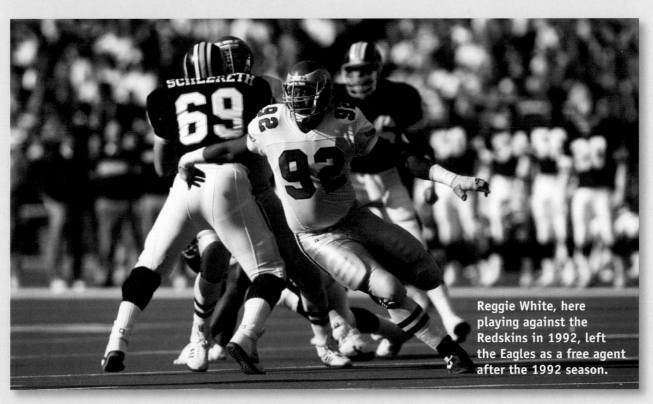

Reggie White, here playing against the Redskins in 1992, left the Eagles as a free agent after the 1992 season.

 20

January 23, 2005

Dawk Crumples Crumpler

Devastating Hit on Falcons Tight End Changes Course of 2004 NFC Title Game

Somehow, Alge Crumpler held onto the football for a 31-yard gain to set up a Falcons touchdown late in the second quarter of the 2004 NFC Championship Game. It didn't matter a bit. Never before or since has a team hit on a 31-yard play given the opposing team so much momentum.

"They did score there," Brian Dawkins says now. "But it didn't matter. We had made a statement. I had delivered a message."

The Falcons trailed the Eagles 14–3 at Lincoln Financial Field with a Super Bowl berth at stake and had a first-and-10 on the Eagles' 41-yard line when Michael Vick spotted Crumpler, his five-time Pro Bowl tight end, steaming down the field inside the 20-yard line.

Dawkins, the seven-time Pro Bowl safety, watched this unfold from down near the 10-yard line. "Going into the game, we knew Mike doesn't look off [receivers] a lot," Dawkins said. "Who he's looking at, he's going to go there with the ball."

Vick shuffled his feet as he threw to Crumpler, and that put some extra air underneath the pass, giving Dawkins more of a head start. Crumpler caught the football at the 14-yard line. As soon as he secured it, Dawkins arrived from the right, running full speed. Crumpler had no idea he was there.

The collision was ferocious. Dawkins came in with his right shoulder and blasted Crumpler so violently that he sent the 265-pound Crumpler flying through the air. Crumpler landed motionless in a pile at the 10-yard line, and Dawkins marched around, looking like some kind of prehistoric warrior celebrating the kill.

Crumpler, who had caught four passes for 49 yards up to that point, was helped off the field. Although he did return later in the game, he didn't catch another pass.

Brian Dawkins celebrates during the NFC Championship Game against the Atlanta Falcons on January 23, 2005.

"Dawk didn't just hit him, he exploded into him," said cornerback Lito Sheppard, who played with Dawkins from 2002 through 2008. "If I hit a guy that size, I'd probably just go backwards."

The Falcons actually scored on the next play, Warrick Dunn running in from 10 yards out. But the tone was set. The Falcons had a touchdown, but the Eagles had command of the game.

"I knew it would be a big hit," Dawkins says now. "I could see it coming because [Crumpler] never saw it coming. If I hadn't anticipated where he was throwing the football, I never would have been in position to make that play."

The Eagles outscored the Falcons 13–0 the rest of the game and won their first NFC title in 24 years. And Dawkins was on his way to his first Super Bowl.

"I remember thinking, *That's what time it is right now. Yes, they got a touchdown, but we all felt the same thing at that moment: We're going to win this game.*

"The Falcons had rushed for over 200 yards the week before [in a playoff win over the Rams], but we were going to show folks what we are all about as a defense."

A few months later, Eagles linebacker Ike Reese signed with the Falcons and became Crumpler's teammate. He didn't waste any time asking him about the play.

"He said, 'Dude, when Dawk hit me, I thought he had knocked all my teeth out,'" Reese said. "He said his face just went numb."

Crumpler wasn't the only person feeling out of it after the play.

"I was woozy after that one," Dawkins said. "If you watch that play, you can see me stumbling around after I hit him. It hurt me, too. I was feeling a little dizzy just from the force of the collision."

But he never left the game. "Of course not," he said. "If I can at all stand, I'm staying in there."

There's no question Dawkins' hit inspired the Eagles. The Falcons had gained 133 yards and scored 10 points on their first four possessions. After the Dawkins hit, they managed just 69 yards and no points on six drives.

"You never want to see anybody get hurt," Sheppard said. "But you could tell that wounded them."

It's not going to be flag football when you are coming across the middle.

—BRIAN DAWKINS

Game Details

Philadelphia Eagles 27 • Atlanta Falcons 10

Eagles	7	7	6	7	**27**
Falcons	0	10	0	0	**10**

Date: January 23, 2005

Team Records: Philadelphia 13–3, Atlanta 11–5

Scoring Plays:

PHI—Levens 4-yard run (Akers PAT)

ATL—Feely 23-yard FG

PHI—C. Lewis 3-yard pass from McNabb (Akers PAT)

ATL—Dunn 10-yard run (Feely PAT)

PHI—Akers 31-yard FG

PHI—Akers 34-yard FG

PHI—C. Lewis 2-yard pass from McNabb (Akers PAT)

It was a playoff catch, it was a playoff hit.

—FALCONS TIGHT END ALGE CRUMPLER

Brian Dawkins

Brian Dawkins started annihilating people as a rookie in 1996 and hasn't let up in 13 seasons. In a city that values thunderous hits above all else, Dawk was the biggest hitter ever.

"Every football fan loves a big hit," Dawkins said, "but it goes way beyond that in Philly. There's a different mentality. There's a desire among the fans to watch us just demolish somebody, and it's passed down from generation to generation.

"Yes, they loved it when Donovan [McNabb] and T.O. were hooking up on big plays and big touchdowns every week. But when you get right down to it, the fans would rather see a big hit than a long run or a big touchdown pass.

"When you can deliver a bone-jarring, snot-bubbling lick on somebody, it's almost like there's something inside the fans that feasts on that. That's the kind of football they want."

And that's the kind of football Dawkins gave Eagles fans before signing with the Broncos in March 2009. He piled up 34 interceptions, 32 forced fumbles, and 21 sacks, but he'll be remembered more than anything for the hits.

Brian Dawkins was the heart, soul, and tenacious spirit of stout Eagles defenses for more than a decade.

"To hit somebody, to *really* hit somebody, there has to be something that's not right inside you—because you're doing something a normal person would not do," Dawkins said. "It takes a different mindset to go out there and really sacrifice your body and unload on an opposing player. You know it's going to hurt, but you're not thinking about that. You just do it."

19

December 10, 1995

Fourth-and-1

Eagles Stuff Emmitt Smith on Surprise Fourth-Down Play, Finally Beat Cowboys

Looking back, it seems preposterous. The Eagles and Cowboys were tied at 17 with less than two and a half minutes left in their critical game at windswept Veterans Stadium in December 1995.

The Cowboys entered the game 10–3 and filled with confidence—understandable, since they had won two Super Bowls in the last four years, they had won seven straight over the Eagles by an average of two touchdowns, and they had beaten the Eagles by 22 points just five weeks earlier. The Eagles were 8–5 and just hoping to sneak into the playoffs.

"They had pretty much manhandled us for years," Eagles defensive tackle Andy Harmon remembers. "They always killed us."

On this day at the Vet, the Cowboys, who had lost all of a 17–3 second-quarter lead, found themselves with fourth-and-1 at their own 29-yard line late in a tie game. The Eagles assumed coach Barry Switzer would send out punter John Jett. Instead, they watched in shock as the Cowboys' offense lined up. From inside their own 30-yard line.

"It surprised us," Eagles Coach Ray Rhodes said after the game. "But when you've been on top as long as they've been on top, you take your chances."

The play call was a no-brainer. Load left. First-ballot Hall of Famer Emmitt Smith gets the ball off tackle.

"Eighty percent of Emmitt's touchdowns with the Cowboys came on that play," Troy Aikman says today.

This time, the Eagles stuffed it for no gain. The only problem was, the play didn't count. The stadium was so loud, nobody realized the two-minute warning was called before the snap. So the Cowboys got another chance, and Switzer didn't hesitate. It came out of a slightly different formation, but he called the same play: load left. And the Eagles stuffed it. Again.

"It's insane that the play didn't work the first time, so they ran the exact same play the second time," Harmon said. "The two plays were identical.

"When we played Dallas, I usually lined up opposite Larry Allen, but since we were in short yardage, I was lining up over [Mark] Tuinei. He came off the ball like a rocket, and I basically jumped around the block and dove in. I got the first penetration, and everybody else came in and stopped Emmitt.

"Then we found out it didn't count and they had another chance. And the exact same thing happened. They ran the exact same play and it developed the exact same way. Tuinei came off the ball like a rocket, I jumped around

Bill Romanowski celebrates after the Eagles defense stopped Emmitt Smith on fourth down with one yard to go in the fourth quarter on December 10, 1995.

the block and got the first penetration, and everybody else came in and stopped Emmitt. It was like instant replay."

The Eagles gained five yards on their next three snaps, and with just over a minute left, Gary Anderson kicked a 42-yard field goal to give the Eagles a 20–17 win and—for the time being—keep the Cowboys from clinching the NFC East title.

"What a great feeling," Harmon says now. "We always had such a struggle against Dallas. They showed no respect for us and our defense by going for it on fourth down. It was huge for us to stop them there and win that game."

Switzer got skewered in Dallas. He had finally lost his mind, the media concluded.

"I remember the headlines," Aikman says. "'Coach Bozo,' with a big picture of Switzer under it. But I absolutely agreed with the call. I was for it.

"The winds were so strong, I just felt a punt wasn't going to help us very much. John had already had a couple very short punts into the wind, and if we punted, Philadelphia would have great field position and a great chance to kick a game-winning field goal.

"Our only chance to win that game was to get a conversion on first down. They made a great play—not once, but twice—and they won the game, but I still believe that was the right call."

Cowboys Hall of Fame running back Emmitt Smith is stuffed at the goal line by Eagles linebacker Kurt Gouvein (54) and defensive tackle Kevin Johnson (94) during the Eagles-Cowboys game at the Vet in 1995. In the fourth quarter, the Eagles stopped Smith on 4th-and-1 deep in Dallas territory with the score tied.

The Eagles went on to reach the postseason and win a wild-card game over the Lions, their only home playoff win during the 19-year span between 1981 through 1999. And although the Cowboys went on to another Super Bowl title, that fourth down stop showed the Eagles that they could play with their hated rivals.

"That play was truly a turning point for us," Harmon said. "If they convert and win the game, everything changes. But it really gave us the confidence we needed going into the end of the season and the playoffs."

> They were the Cowboys. They thought they could get a first down in any situation.
>
> —EAGLES LINEBACKER WILLIAM THOMAS

Game Details

Philadelphia Eagles 20 • Dallas Cowboys 17

Eagles	3	3	8	6	20
Cowboys	7	10	0	0	17

Date: December 10, 1995

Team Records: Philadelphia 8–5, Dallas 10–3

Scoring Plays:

PHI—Anderson 42-yard FG

DAL—Smith 10-yard run (Boniol PAT)

DAL—Boniol 21-yard FG

DAL—Brown 65-yard interception return (Boniol PAT)

PHI—Anderson 27-yard FG

PHI—Watters 1-yard run (Barnett pass from Peete)

PHI—Anderson 38-yard FG

PHI—Anderson 42-yard FG

Containing Michael Irvin

On the same day the Eagles stopped the Cowboys on consecutive fourth-and-1 plays late in the fourth quarter, another even more significant story began developing: Eagles head coach Ray Rhodes told rookie cornerback Bobby Taylor to cover future Hall of Famer Michael Irvin.

"For me, as a rookie, it was a little scary but challenging," Taylor said. "I knew I had to step up big time."

Earlier that season, in a 34–12 Dallas rout, Irvin torched the Eagles with eight catches for 115 yards and a touchdown. So Rhodes turned to Taylor, a second-round pick from Notre Dame.

This time, with Taylor blanketing him, Irvin caught three passes for 40 yards and got nowhere near the end zone. Taylor remained glued to Irvin over the next four years until Irvin retired after the 1999 season. In those six match-ups, Irvin caught just 22 passes for 315 yards and one touchdown.

"Whenever people look back on my career, one of the first things they mention is me covering Michael," Taylor said. "After that first game, he knew when we played, he had to pack a lunch, and, of course, I knew I had to pack a lunch."

Taylor grew up a Cowboys fan, and the games in Texas Stadium were always extra special.

"No doubt I established a name for myself by playing against Michael," Taylor said. "All young players should strive for that. That's how you have to do it. You have to go up against a great player to make yourself known."

18

December 26, 1960

Dean's Fourth-Quarter Touchdown Gives Eagles 1960 NFL Championship

Van Brocklin Changes Play, Rookie Backup Scores Game-Winner

Norm Van Brocklin's play call was exactly what Ted Dean expected. Billy Barnes would get the football, and Dean would block.

The Eagles trailed Vince Lombardi's Packers 13–10 with five minutes to go in the 1960 NFL Championship Game at Franklin Field, but they were just five yards from the end zone and five yards from a likely NFL title.

"With so much on the line, I knew Barnes would get the ball," Dean says today. "He was a good runner, and I was just a rookie. And that's what Van Brocklin called in the huddle."

Barnes was a 25-year-old veteran who was picked to the NFL All-Star team in each of his first three NFL seasons and had already scored 24 career touchdowns. Dean was a 22-year-old rookie who had scored only three touchdowns

(none of them rushing) and was only playing because Clarence Peaks—who had been having a terrific season—broke his leg in a game against the Redskins six weeks earlier.

"Dean took over and played better than his numbers suggest," says NFL historian Ray Didinger. "He only averaged 2.8 yards per carry, but he did a decent job. He was a good receiver, maybe a better receiver than a pure runner."

Nonetheless, somewhere between the huddle and the line of scrimmage, Van Brocklin changed his mind. With time running out on the 1960 season, Van Brocklin decided to hand off to Dean and not Barnes.

"We were walking up to the line and he yelled out, 'Switch,' and changed the play,'" Dean said. "I can't speculate why he did it, and I never had the opportunity to ask him. He had faith in

Ted Dean (35) heads for a big hole and a touchdown in the fourth quarter of the NFL Championship Game against the Green Bay Packers on December 26, 1960 in Philadelphia.

me. He knew my potential and put his trust in me. I was elated, of course—I wanted to be the one running over the goal line.

"I had fumbled earlier in the game, and I rarely ever fumbled. Van Brocklin knew I was still hot from fumbling, so maybe that's why he gave me the ball," said Dean.

Why did Van Brocklin change the play? Nobody knows.

"Van Brocklin saw something at the line. To this day nobody knows what he saw," Didinger said. "but he checked out and called the sweep to Dean."

Dean's earlier fumble was at the Eagles' own 20-yard line after a 10-yard gain. Bill Forester recovered for the Packers, leading to Paul Hornung's short field goal. But Dean also saved a touchdown with a diving tackle of Max McGee after a 35-yard run on a fake punt.

"He was gone, he was gone," Dean said. "I was hoping to get him farther up the field, but I was blocked. He was actually a step beyond me when I tackled him, and he probably didn't even know I was there. All he could see was the goal line. If I hadn't gotten him, that was a touchdown."

Quarterback Norm Van Brocklin got the call, handoff to Billy Barnes, but something told the veteran QB to give the go to running back Ted Dean instead.

And after the Packers took a 13–10 lead on Bart Starr's seven-yard touchdown pass to McGee early in the fourth quarter, Dean fielded Hornung's kickoff at the 3-yard line and returned the ball 58 yards to the Packers' 39-yard line to give the Eagles one final chance.

Eight plays later, on second-and-goal from the 5-yard line, Dean ran a sweep left behind a block from guard Gerry Huth for the game-winning touchdown.

"I put my head down like a battering ram, ran behind a block behind Gerry Huth, and I was in," Dean said. "I wasn't touched until just before I got into the end zone."

Dean holds the distinction of scoring the winning touchdown in the only playoff game that Starr or Hall of Fame coach Vince Lombardi ever lost, as well as the last NFL championship the Eagles won.

But it never was a big deal to him. "I was never the type of player who wanted credit," he said. "If the team won, I won. If the team lost, I lost. It was a thrill to score that touchdown, but if anybody else had scored it and we had won, it would have been just as big a thrill."

Game Details

Philadelphia Eagles 17 • Green Bay Packers 13

Eagles	0	10	0	7	**17**
Packers	3	3	0	7	**13**

Date: December 26, 1960
Team Records: Philadelphia 10–2, Green Bay 8–4
Scoring Plays:
GB—Hornung 20-yard FG
GB—Hornung 23-yard FG
PHI—McDonald 35-yard pass from Van Brocklin (Watson PAT)
PHI—Walston 15-yard FG
GB—McGee 7-yard pass from Starr (Hornung PAT)
PHI—Dean 5-yard run (Walston PAT)

The Drought

When he scored the winning touchdown against the Packers to give the Eagles the 1960 NFL title, Ted Dean never dreamed the Eagles would still be looking for another title 49 years later.

"It's been quite a while," Dean said.

Heading into 2009, only the Lions and Cardinals had gone longer than the Eagles without winning an NFL title. The Lions last won a championship in 1957 and the Cards last did it in 1947—against the Eagles.

Among teams from the other major U.S. sports, only the Cubs (1908), Indians (1948), Sacramento Kings (1951), San Francisco Giants (1954), and Atlanta Hawks (1958) have gone longer since their last championship.

"They've been knocking at the door so many times," Hall of Famer Tommy McDonald says today. "They've gotten it about halfway open a few times, but they just haven't been able to get all the way through and win that Super Bowl.

"They've had their share of great players, and that's where it starts. But to win a championship, the right things have to happen. You have to be healthy. You have to get the breaks. The ball has to bounce your way and not bounce the other guy's way. There is a lot that goes into winning it all."

Since the Eagles' last title, 15 NFL franchises have won a championship. Nearly half the league.

"I am kind of surprised they haven't won again," Bednarik said. "When I die, I'll be up in heaven, and I'll do what I can to see they win one."

Making a touchdown wasn't the best part. Winning the game was the most important thing.
—EAGLES RUNNING BACK TED DEAN

17

November 20, 1988

Miracle II

Simmons Scoops Up Blocked Field Goal, Returns for Touchdown in OT Win Over Giants

Clyde Simmons had heard the sound before, that thud of a football being blocked. Usually, he was on the other side.

Just a week earlier, the Eagles' Pro Bowl defensive end had blocked a game-winning field goal attempt by the Steelers' Gary Anderson in a 27–26 Eagles win, one of his seven blocked kicks in seven years with the Eagles.

On this day, that sound came from a different direction. The Eagles and Giants were tied 17–17 in overtime when safety Terry Hoage's interception of Jeff Hostetler led to a 31-yard game-winning field goal attempt by Eagles kicker Luis Zendejas. But Giants Hall of Famer Lawrence Taylor rushed from the right side and blocked Zendejas' kick.

"You know the sound when a kick gets blocked," Simmons said. "I had heard it before. So I kind of knew where to look for the ball, but then it bounced right to me."

Simmons secured the ball and rumbled 15 yards into the end zone six minutes into overtime. The Eagles won 23–17 and moved into a tie for first place in the NFC East, which they went on to win for the first time in eight years.

"The funny thing about that play is everyone told me it was partially my fault the kick got blocked," Simmons said. "It came from my side. I thought I did my job, but everyone said it was on me."

Had Simmons recovered in front of the 13-yard line, the original line of scrimmage, he would have been unable to advance the ball, and the Giants would have gotten the ball back.

"I just spun around, grabbed it, and ran to the end zone," Simmons said. "I was going to do whatever it took to get it in there. We had played too good that day to lose the game. I remember when I finally got in the end zone, the guys piled on me. Big Dog [Reggie White] was right on top of me, and I could barely breathe."

Simmons didn't run straight for the end zone. He had to elude a couple Giants defenders along the way.

"For him to be 6'5" and be able to scoop that ball up— a lot of skill players can't make that play," linebacker Seth Joyner said. "To collect himself, bend down, scoop up the ball, dodge one or two guys, make one or two guys miss, and get into the end zone, for him to pull that off at such a

Fearsome Giants linebacker Lawrence Taylor may have blocked the field goal, but it was Eagles lineman Clyde Simmons who got the loose ball and returned it for a touchdown.

Clyde Simmons

When you're a ninth-round draft pick out of Western Carolina, it's easy to get overlooked. And when the team that finally does draft you already has a player at your position who's the greatest ever, it's even easier.

Sometimes, people can get caught up in the mystique," Simmons said. "They don't get motivated as much when they don't get the attention. I never let that get to me. I remember the one year I was third in the league in sacks and didn't go to the Pro Bowl. That bothered me at first, but my teammates always supported me. That meant more to me than any outside attention."

That year was 1989, and Simmons was snubbed for Pro Bowl honors despite 15½ sacks, third-most of any NFL defensive end. That also started a four-year stretch in which Simmons recorded 55 sacks, the most of any player in the NFL. One more even than legendary teammate Reggie White. When Simmons retired, he ranked 11th in NFL history with 121 ½ sacks. He's one of the greatest defensive ends in NFL history (even if few people realize it).

"I never needed to be in the spotlight," Simmons said. "We had enough great players, and we used that to challenge each other. Every time Reggie got a sack, I wanted to get a sack. Every time somebody made a play, it made somebody else want to make a play. I think that's what made our defense so great. We all had so much personal pride."

After recognizing the unmistakable sound of a blocked kick when playing on the field goal kicking unit, Clyde Simmons alertly hunted down the ball, scooped it up, and chugged 15 yards into the end zone to give the Eagles an overtime win against the Giants.

critical time in such a critical game, that was just an unbelievable play for a guy his size."

The game took place 10 years and a day after another unforgettable Eagles win at Giants Stadium. In "the Miracle of the Meadowlands," Herman Edwards scooped up a Giants fumble in the closing seconds and returned it for a touchdown. This one became Miracle II.

"What a play that was," Eagles head coach Buddy Ryan says now. "We were going to beat them either way—make the field goal or have Clyde pick it up and run it in. We just never did it the easy way. But we did beat the Giants every which way."

The Eagles beat the Giants twice that season, giving them the advantage in a tiebreaker over their rival just up the New Jersey Turnpike and their first division title in eight years when both teams finished 10–6.

"Every year when we went into Giants Stadium, I felt the percentages were against us," quarterback Randall Cunningham said. "That year I said, 'The hell with it. We're going to beat them.' When I saw Clyde run that ball into the end zone, tears started welling up in my eyes. It was a feeling I hadn't felt since I'd been there."

Game Details

Philadelphia Eagles 23 • New York Giants 17 (OT)

Eagles	7	3	0	7	6	**23**
Giants	7	3	7	0	0	**17**

Date: November 20, 1988

Team Records: Philadelphia 6–5, New York 7–4

Scoring Plays:

PHI—Cunningham 1-yard run (Zendejas PAT)

NYG—Robinson 62-yard pass from Simms (McFadden PAT)

PHI—Zendejas 37-yard FG

NYG—McFadden 21-yard FG

NYG—Baker 9-yard pass from Simms (McFadden PAT)

PHI—Carter fumble recovery in end zone (Zendejas PAT)

PHI—Simmons 15-yard return of blocked FG

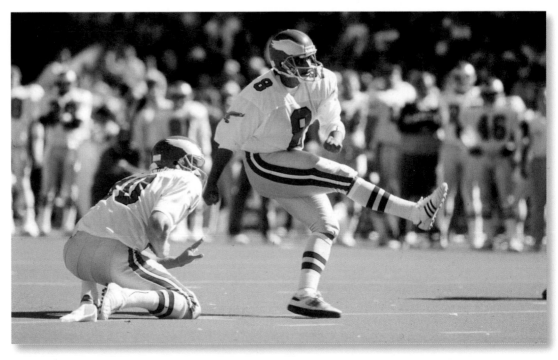

When Luis Zendejas' kick was blocked by Lawrence Taylor, Clyde Simmons picked up the ball and returned it for a touchdown.

16

December 26, 1960

A Taylor-Made Tackle

Bednarik Sits on Packer RB as Eagles Hold Off Packers in 1960 Championship Game

Eight yards were all that remained between Jim Taylor, the end zone, and Vince Lombardi's first NFL title with the Green Bay Packers. Eight yards and Chuck Bednarik. Two future Hall of Famers were about to collide with a NFL title on the line. Does it get any better than that?

"Taylor was a tough one—a great running back, one of the best ever," Bednarik said. "That whole team was great. But I knew I had to make the play there or we would lose the game. I was the only one standing between him and the end zone, so I knew I had to tackle him. I gave him a big bear-hug tackle up high and wrestled him to the ground."

And there they both stayed until a moment before the clock hit 0:00.

"It was one of those see-saw games," Bednarik said. "We led at halftime by a couple [10–6]. They came back in the fourth quarter [to lead 13–10], and then we came back again to lead 17–13. But we knew, and everyone in the place knew, with Bart Starr and Taylor and all those other guys they had, the Packers still were going to take one more shot."

Earlier in the game, Bednarik had knocked out Paul Hornung, Green Bay's other Hall of Fame running back. Hornung came into the game with a bad shoulder, and a hit by Bednarik made it worse.

On that final play, Starr first looked to the end zone. When he couldn't find an open receiver, he dumped the ball off to Taylor and hoped for the best.

"Everyone must have been covered downfield," Bednarik said. "Taylor caught the little swing pass, put his head down and started running. The clock was ticking. A couple of our guys tried to tackle him, but he was a big guy, tough to bring down."

Taylor bounced off four different Eagles and got to the 8-yard line when Bednarik hauled him to the ground.

"He's running with a full head of steam, and your heart is in your throat," said long-time *Philadelphia Daily News* Eagles writer Ray Didinger, who was seated in the end zone that day. "Your only hope is that No. 60 can make the play."

Of course, he did.

"That last play was something," wide receiver Tommy McDonald said. "That was Chuck. He tackles Jimmy Taylor

Chuck Bednarik (No. 60) tackles Green Bay's Jim Taylor to seal the 17–13 win for the Eagles in the 1960 NFL Championship Game on December 26, 1960.

and sits on him and counts the seconds down. I don't know everything that happened, but I knew Chuck wasn't going to let Jimmy get up until the game was over."

Footage from the NFL Films vault shows the play wasn't quite as dramatic as has been reported through the years. Bednarik didn't quite sit on Taylor until time ran out, but either way, the Packers wouldn't have time for another play. In the end, it came down to two great players, one great play.

"On the ground, I could see the time ticking away on the clock—four, three, two, one, zero," Bednarik said.

Chuck Bednarik celebrates after defeating the Green Bay Packers in the NFC Championship Game at Franklin Field on December 26, 1960.

Game Details

Philadelphia Eagles 17 • Green Bay Packers 13

Eagles	0	10	0	7	**17**
Packers	3	3	0	7	**13**

Date: December 26, 1960

Team Records: Philadelphia 10–2, Green Bay 8–4

Scoring Plays:

GB—Hornung 20-yard FG

GB—Hornung 23-yard FG

PHI—McDonald 35-yard pass from Van Brocklin (Walston PAT)

PHI—Walston 15-yard FG

GB—McGee 7-yard pass from Starr (Hornung PAT)

PHI—Dean 5-yard run (Walston PAT)

"That's when I got up, and I said the same thing I said [on the hit on Frank Gifford against the Giants], 'This f––ing game is over.'"

Lombardi and Starr never lost another postseason game. The Packers won the 1961 NFL title, the first of five in a seven-year span. As of 2008, the 1960 championship was the Eagles' last. But for one day, for one moment nearly half a century ago, the Eagles ruled the National Football League.

"They had a great team, and Lombardi was the perfect coach for them," Bednarik said. "But we had a good team, too. I wouldn't say we were the best team that year, but we were the best team that day."

> **T**aylor was not an easy man to tackle. He was a big, tough son of a gun who would not go down easily.
>
> **—HALL OF FAMER CHUCK BEDNARIK**

The Dutchman

Norm Van Brocklin didn't want to come to Philadelphia. He didn't want anything to do with Philadelphia. Yet that's exactly where the Rams traded him after the 1957 season. Only after NFL Commissioner and Eagles founder Bert Bell promised Van Brocklin that he would eventually replace Buck Shaw as head coach did he accept the trade. Then, all Van Brocklin did in his three years with the Eagles was take one of the NFL's worst teams and turn it into a championship team.

"He was a great quarterback before he got to Philly," wide receiver Tommy McDonald said. "He was great with the Rams. We were lucky to get him."

During his nine years with the Rams, "The Dutchman" made six Pro Bowl teams and threw the game-winning touchdown in the 1951 NFL Championship victory against the Browns. Nine years later, he led the Eagles to the 1960 Championship over the Packers, the only postseason loss of Vince Lombardi's career.

"We had a good team," said Chuck Bednarik. "But we had a great quarterback. We would have never won without Van Brocklin."

Van Brocklin never did become Eagles head coach. Bell died in 1959, and his promise died with him. Van Brocklin coached 13 years with the Vikings and Falcons before retiring in 1974.

"I'll tell you one thing about Van Brocklin," McDonald said. "He wasn't just a great quarterback, he was a great leader. He helped everyone on the team be better. We knew if we had Van Brocklin, we had a chance to win any game."

Although Norm Van Brocklin was at first reluctant to come to Philadelphia from the Rams, his arrival marked a turning point for the franchise.

15

January 3, 1993

Reggie Sacks the Saints

Hall of Famer Highlights Fourth-Quarter Playoff Rally with Safety

Reggie White had never won a championship—not in high school at the Howard School of Academics and Technology in Chattanooga, not at the University of Tennessee, not with the USFL's Memphis Showboats, and not in his first seven seasons with the Eagles.

By 1992, he had established himself as one of the greatest defensive players in NFL history. He had 124 sacks in just eight seasons, an average of 15 ½ per season. With seven seasons to go, he already ranked second in NFL history.

He had the reputation. He had the records. He had two sack titles. But he didn't have a championship to show for it.

"We talked about that all the time," said long-time Eagles teammate Eric Allen, a five-time Pro Bowl cornerback. "Those teams in 1988, 1989, and 1990, we thought we had

a chance, but we didn't even win a playoff game. In 1992, that was going to be the year we finally did it. We really believed we had a chance."

Those 1992 Eagles won their last four regular-season games and roared into the postseason as one of the hottest teams in football. But they found themselves trailing the Saints 20–10 early in the fourth quarter of their wild-card playoff game at the Superdome. White was facing another off-season without a Super Bowl title, without even a postseason win.

That's when one of the greatest comebacks in NFL playoff history began. Randall Cunningham's 35-yard touchdown pass to Fred Barnett and a six-yard touchdown run by Heath Sherman gave the Eagles a 24–20 lead. The Saints got the ball back deep in their own end, and the Eagles' defense smelled blood. They knew they were one huge defensive

Reggie White sacks quarterback Bobby Hebert of the New Orleans Saints for a safety in the Superdome in the 1992
NFC Wild Card Game on January 3, 1993 in New Orleans. The Eagles defeated the Saints, 36–20.

play away from taking command and winning their first playoff game in 12 years. It was White's time.

"Reggie had the ability to get his right hand underneath the tackle's armpit and just throw him down, and he did that move right then," Allen recalled. "It was a great move."

Saints quarterback Bobby Hebert, standing in the end zone looking for a receiver, never had a chance. White threw 6'6", 285-pound offensive tackle Stan Brock into Hebert, then grabbed Hebert's feet and yanked him to the ground.

"I used a bull rush and just knocked him backwards," White said after the game. "He was right there and I pulled him down."

White signaled safety before the refs did. The Eagles led 26–20 and had all the momentum. The Saints were done.

"It was a great move and great penetration," Allen said. "Hebert had no chance to escape. Reggie just swarmed him."

A Roger Ruzek field goal and Allen's 18-yard interception return for a touchdown gave the Eagles 26 fourth-quarter points and a 36–20 win. Going into 2009, it remains the second-highest fourth quarter score in NFL playoff history and the biggest since 1934.

"I made sure to go over and say, 'Great play, Reg,' because with Reggie, whenever he made a big play, nobody ever said anything to him," Allen said. "Everybody expected it. Those were the kinds of plays everybody expected.

"I remember in 1988, my rookie year, he made a great play and I jumped on him celebrating, and after the game he said, 'EA, you're the first guy who's ever expressed his excitement about a play I made.' I said, 'What are you talking about?' But everybody took him for granted. He made those kinds of plays all the time. It was like, 'Okay, Reggie made another great play.' It wasn't that we didn't appreciate him, we were just so used to it. That time against the Saints, I made sure I said something to him because that was such a big play for him and such a big play for our team. That really put a stamp on a great comeback. It was a great play by one of the greatest to ever play the game."

> **I**t was a typical Reggie sack. He picked the guy up and threw him around like a rag doll.
>
> —EAGLES LINEBACKER SETH JOYNER

Game Details

Philadelphia Eagles 36 • New Orleans Saints 20

Eagles	7	0	3	26	**36**
Saints	7	10	3	0	**20**

Date: January 3, 1993

Team Records: Philadelphia 11–5, New Orleans 12–4

Scoring Plays:

NO—Heyward 1-yard run (Andersen PAT)

PHI—Barnett 57-yard pass from Cunningham (Ruzek PAT)

NO—Andersen 35-yard FG

NO—Early 7-yard pass from Hebert (Andersen PAT)

NO—Andersen 42-yard FG

PHI—Ruzek 40-yard FG

PHI—Barnett 35-yard pass from Cunningham (Ruzek PAT)

PHI—Sherman 6-yard run (Ruzek PAT)

PHI—Safety, White sacked Hebert in end zone

PHI—Ruzek, 39-yard FG

PHI—Allen, 18-yard interception return (Ruzek PAT)

Jerome's Locker

When Jerome Brown and his 12-year-old nephew died in a car accident just before 1992 training camp, it shattered an Eagles team with Super Bowl aspirations.

"Jerome was the glue that held us together," cornerback Eric Allen said.

In just five NFL seasons, Brown had already made two Pro Bowl teams and recorded 29 ½ sacks as a defensive tackle. But the loss went much deeper than his play on the field.

"He was a great player, but he was so much more than that," Allen said. "He was a guy who was able to talk to everyone. The roughest, toughest guy on any team, he'd have their respect. The rookie who came in from Montana or Utah and had no sense of urban life, he'd make him feel comfortable. The minister who came to talk to the team. He was comfortable in any situation."

The Eagles retired Brown's No. 99, but the players were looking for a more personal way to remember him. So they elected to leave his locker intact that season, and when the Eagles traveled to New Orleans for their wild-card playoff game, Brown's locker made the trip as well, with all his stuff inside it.

"We had a lot of great players on that team, but he held it all together," Allen said. "And we needed a piece of that. It was comforting having his locker there with us. Things that seemed difficult or tough didn't seem so difficult or tough when Jerome's locker was with us."

Reggie White, Clyde Simmons (partially obsured), and Seth Joyner hold up former Eagles lineman Jerome Brown's retired jersey, No. 99, at a ceremony prior to a game against the New Orleans Saints at Veterans Stadium.

14

November 15, 2004

The Play That Went On Forever

McNabb's 14-Second Scramble, 60-yard Bomb to Mitchell to Stun Cowboys

We all knew Donovan McNabb could run forever, and we all knew he could throw the ball a mile. In a game against the Cowboys in 2004, he did both. At the same time.

The Eagles led the hated Cowboys 28–14 at Texas Stadium but faced a third-and-10 on their own 25-yard line with three minutes left in the second quarter. McNabb dropped back to pass but found himself immediately under siege by defensive tackle Leonardo Carson, who blasted untouched past left guard Artis Hicks and wrapped his arms around McNabb before McNabb broke free with a 360-degree spin move.

Then McNabb began scrambling. And he didn't stop for 14 seconds. Seeing Carson and defensive end Eric Ogbogu to his left, McNabb dashed to his right looking for a receiver, and he kept going until he was only a few feet from the right sideline.

"T.O. was the only guy on that side of the field," McNabb said. "But he was covered on a shallow cross, and I couldn't get my feet together to throw anyway. So I just started running the other way."

McNabb slipped on the numeral 1 that marks the 10-yard line and nearly lost his footing, then began racing left to right, retreating as deep as the 7-yard line as he tried to figure out what to do next.

"I blocked somebody and turned around looking for Donovan and saw him going the other way," guard Jermane Mayberry said. "Hey, how did you get over there?"

Offensive linemen were scattered randomly and blocking anybody they could find. Mayberry annihilated La'Roi Glover and right tackle Jon Runyan took care of Ogbogu, freeing McNabb to race across the field to the left sideline.

"It was tiring," McNabb said. "But the guys just continued to work. Scramble drill is something we paid a lot of attention to. That's a dream for offensive linemen, getting clean-up shots."

McNabb was in a full sprint down the left sideline when he reached the 20-yard line. He pump-faked to try and lose two defenders speeding toward him, then, moments before he reached the line of scrimmage, he spotted Freddie Mitchell streaking across the field right to left with a step on cornerback Nate Jones down at the 30-yard line. Mitchell had consistently complained that he

Donovan McNabb eludes Leonardo Carson on his way to throwing a 60-yard pass in a Monday night game against the Cowboys in Irving, Texas on November 15, 2004. The Eagles won 49–21.

didn't get the ball enough. He would only play 10 more NFL games. This time, the ball went his way.

"I saw Todd [Pinkston] going across the field," McNabb said. "But then at the last second I saw Freddie getting open."

The problem was getting the ball to him, 65 yards away.

"When we worked out Donovan (as a college senior) at the Carrier Dome, it was at the end of a long day, and people had been putting him through every kind of drill, and he was just about exhausted," head coach Andy Reid said. "People from other teams were actually leaving—I think they felt sorry for Donovan at that point. But [former offensive coordinator] Rod Dowhower had him do exactly that—throw on the move, from difficult positions, as far as he could throw it. And it was unbelievable, really. After all he'd been through that day, he was flinging that thing 60 yards. So we knew he could do that."

Five years later, McNabb did it in a game. He threw across his body while his momentum carried him out of bounds before the ball came down.

"I just tried to turn my shoulders to get it deep," McNabb. "It was shocking to me to get it out there that far because your body is going one way and your arm is going another way."

But the throw was perfect. Mitchell made the catch at the Dallas 22-yard line and picked up seven more yards before Jones tackled him at the 15. The 60-yard catch was the longest of Mitchell's career. From snap to tackle, it took 18.2 seconds.

"I was running a decoy route to free somebody else up," Mitchell says now. "All of a sudden, Donovan's running around, so I'm going for the gusto. I'm going for the big play, and I broke down the field. I didn't think he'd throw it to me. He hadn't thrown to me the whole game.

Eagles wide receiver Freddie Mitchell, shown here catching a pass from Donovan McNabb in the Eagles' 2004 playoff win over the Vikings at the Linc, was on the receiving end of McNabb's 60-yard bomb following a 14-second scramble a few weeks earlier against the Cowboys at Texas Stadium.

Game Details

Philadelphia Eagles 49 • Dallas Cowboys 21

Eagles	7	28	7	7	**49**
Cowboys	0	14	7	0	**21**

Date: November 15, 2004

Team Records: Philadelphia 7–1, Dallas 3–5

Scoring Plays:

PHI—Owens 59-yard pass from McNabb (Akers PAT)

PHI—Levens 4-yard run (Akers PAT)

DAL—Witten 29-yard pass from Testaverde (Cundiff PAT)

PHI—Owens 27-yard pass from McNabb (Akers PAT)

PHI—Pinkston 59-yard pass from McNabb (Akers PAT)

DAL—Witten 24-yard pass from Testaverde (Cundiff PAT)

PHI—Westbrook 1-yard run (Akers PAT)

DAL—George 15-yard run (Cundiff PAT)

PHI—Owens 16-yard pass from McNabb (Akers PAT)

PHI—Sheppard 101-yard interception return (Akers PAT)

But he had the arm to get it there. I got open, and I made the catch."

Mitchell, who was quick to say that he didn't get the ball enough, got up and pointed to an imaginary wristwatch, telling the world, "It's about time." Then, slipping into his self-appointed role as the People's Champ, he donned his phantom WWE wrestling title belt as the stunned crowd watched in silence.

Mitchell's catch set up a Brian Westbrook touchdown run that helped the Eagles score 28 second-quarter points, the most the Cowboys have ever allowed in a quarter. The Eagles rebounded from their only meaningful loss of the 2004 Super Bowl season a week earlier in Pittsburgh to win, 49–21.

"That play shows how determined Donovan is," Hicks said. "He catches a lot of grief from people, but he never gives up on anything, and that play exhibited that."

Beating the Cowboys

From 1991 through 1998, the Eagles won only five of 18 games against their most-hated rival. Then Andy Reid arrived. And in the next 10 years, the Eagles went 14–6 against Dallas, with eight of the wins by 22 or more points. By 2008, Reid had beaten the Cowboys more than any coach in NFL history.

"Andy Reid is the guy who ruined the decade for the Cowboys," Ravens head coach John Harbaugh said. "Think about it—they've been trying to get back to where they were the whole decade, and the Eagles have been the ones keeping them from getting there. They've stuck daggers in the Cowboys year after year."

The Cowboys won three Super Bowls in the 1990s, beating the Eagles in the playoffs in two of those three seasons. But from 1999 through 2008, the Cowboys reached the postseason only four times and didn't win a playoff game.

"Why is that?" said Harbaugh, who spent nine years as an assistant coach with the Eagles. "Because what Andy Reid and his program stand for is the opposite of what the Cowboys stand for. The Cowboys are a star system. It's all about building around individuals first and collecting talent, collecting great players. Andy has always been about building a team. And over the long haul, it's a team sport, and one of the greatest examples of that is what's happened with the Eagles and the Cowboys over the last 10 years. The Cowboys stand for everything that's wrong in the NFL."

I don't think any other quarterback could have made that play.

—EAGLES GUARD ARTIS HICKS

13

December 18, 1949

Skladany Touchdown Clinches 1949 NFL Title

Obscure Rookie Blocks Punt, Recovers, and Scores in Win Over Rams

Leo Skladany played eight NFL games in his life. He started one. He was out of football before his 24th birthday. He would have been one of the most obscure players in NFL history. Except for the fact that he made one of its biggest plays in NFL history.

The Eagles had won the 1948 NFL Championship over the Cards, and a year later were seeking to join the 1940 and 1941 Chicago Bears as only the second team in history to win consecutive league-championship games.

The only blip in an 11–1 regular season was a 38–21 Week 4 loss to the Bears at Wrigley Field. Nonetheless, the 1949 NFL Championship Game was played in Los Angeles, the first league title game played on the West Coast. Because Eagles coach Greasy Neale was afraid to fly, the Eagles took a three-day train trip out to L.A. with a stop in Albuquerque to practice on the way. The

Eagles had hammered the Rams at home 38–14 six weeks earlier, but in the driving rain and on a sloppy field, the championship game was much closer.

Eagles quarterback Tommy Thompson only completed five passes, but one was a 31-yard touchdown to future Hall of Famer Pete Pihos that gave the Eagles a 7–0 lead in the second quarter. It was still 7–0 in the third quarter at rainy, muddy Los Angeles Coliseum when Hall of Famer Bob Waterfield dropped back to punt near the Rams' goal line.

The snap from center Don Paul was high, and Waterfield had to jump up just to get his hands on the ball. Skladany raced in and not only blocked the punt and recovered it at the 2-yard line, but he rambled into the end zone for the clinching touchdown.

"Earlier in the game, he came close to blocking one, but that time he came full bore and, by golly, he got that punt," All-Pro lineman Al Wistert recalled. "He was a first-year man and we weren't

Coach Earl "Greasy" Neale, third from left, discusses a play, December 25, 1947 with three of his stellar performers (left to right) halfback Steve Van Buren, tackle Al Wistert, and quarterback Tommy Thompson.

expecting him to make that kind of play, but he did and it was wonderful."

Through 2008, Skladany was one of only two players in NFL history to block a punt and recover it for a touchdown in the postseason. The Dolphins' Charlie Babb did it in a conference semifinal win over the Browns in 1972.

"I just took a straight line to Waterfield," Skladany said in the *Eagles Encyclopedia*, written by Ray Didinger and

Robert S. Lyons. "I threw myself in the air, and I was lucky enough to get the ball just as it was coming off his foot. The ball stuck in the mud. That's how deep it was. I just grabbed it and skidded across the goal line. The other players all mobbed me. What a feeling."

The Eagles won 14–0, thanks in large part to Hall of Famer Steve Van Buren, who rushed 31 times for a playoff-record 196 yards; thanks to their defense, which limited

Eagles halfback Frank Reagan (40) intercepts a pass by quarterback Bob Waterfield of the Los Angeles Rams on his own three-yard line in the second half of the NFL Championship Game in Los Angeles on December 18, 1949.

The Dynasty

Long before Jim Johnson and his vast array of blitz packages, decades before brilliant defensive minds like Emmitt Thomas, Bud Carson, and Buddy Ryan, the Eagles boasted one of the greatest defenses in NFL history.

The Eagles beat the Cards 7–0 and the Rams 14–0 in the 1948 and 1949 NFL Championship Games, allowing the Cards 99 yards and the Rams 119, the two lowest totals in NFL or NFC Championship Game history.

"That Eagles team of the postwar era is one of the greatest teams ever," NFL historian Ray Didinger said. "Think about back-to-back shutouts in the NFL Championship Game against a Cardinals team that went 11–1 and an explosive Rams team that had two Hall of Fame quarterbacks and two Hall of Fame receivers and led the league in points. That's an incredible accomplishment."

The 1948 and 1949 Eagles went 20–3–1, outscoring their opponents by an average of 31–13. The Eagles remain the only franchise to record shutouts in consecutive title games.

The 1947 Eagles lost to the Cards 29–21 in the NFL title game after beating the Steelers 21–0 in a playoff game. No other team has recorded a postseason shutout in two consecutive seasons. The legendary Eagles did it in three straight seasons.

"It was great knowing that everybody was trying to defeat the defending champions, and no matter how hard they tried, they couldn't knock us off our perch," Steve Van Buren said. "I was happy for [Coach] Greasy Neale, and to win it for the city and my teammates."

Neale, Van Buren, Pete Pihos, Alex Wojciechowicz, and Chuck Bednarik are all enshrined in the Pro Football Hall of Fame.

the Rams to an all-time postseason-low 21 rushing yards and just 119 total yards; and thanks to the weather, which limited the vaunted Rams passing attack to just 98 yards.

And they won because of an unknown kid who was in the right place at the right time, one of the biggest moments in franchise history.

"I would have played for nothing that day," said Skladany, who died in 2003. "Today, it's all about the money. Back in those days, football was football."

> **T**hat was probably the biggest play in the game.
>
> —EAGLES OFFENSIVE LINEMAN AL WISTERT

Game Details

Philadelphia Eagles 14 • Los Angeles Rams 0

Eagles	0	7	7	0	**14**
Rams	0	0	0	0	**0**

Date: December 18, 1949

Team Records: Philadelphia 11–1, Los Angeles 8–2–2

Scoring Plays:

PHI—Pihos 31-yard pass from Thompson (Patton PAT)

PHI—Skladany 2-yard blocked punt return (Patton PAT)

12

December 3, 1989

The Punt

Versatile Quarterback Blasts 91-Yard Punt, Third-Longest in NFL History

If you attended Eagles training camp in West Chester, Pennsylvania in the late 1980s and early 1990s, you would have seen quarterback Randall Cunningham amazing his teammates, goofing around by booting 60-yard punts and 50-yard field goals. On a wind-swept November day in 1989 at Giants Stadium, he did it for real.

"It's funny," Cunningham says today. "I'm watching a game [recently] and I see Jeff Feagles still punting for the Giants, and I thought about that punt back in 1989. Jeff is probably one of the greatest punters ever, and when he came to Philly we always talked about that punt. He would always tell me how I should be a punter."

That day at the Meadowlands, regular Eagles punter John Teltschik was unavailable after going on injured reserve with a knee injury. His replacement, Max Runager, was struggling. So after a failed third down, coach Buddy Ryan told Cunningham to stay on the field and punt.

His kick traveled 91 yards, at the time the second-longest in NFL history and still third-longest ever, going

into the 2009 season. Not only did his punt dazzle fans and teammates, it set up the winning touchdown in a 24–17 victory.

"That was some deal," Eagles head coach Buddy Ryan says today. "You know, he did practice it a lot. He said he wanted to go out there. So I said, 'Go ahead,' and when he kicked it, I thought he knocked it out of the damn stadium."

With the score tied 17–17 in the fourth quarter, the Eagles were backed up at their 3-yard line. Cunningham, standing near the back of the end zone, launched his punt into the 25-mph wind, and it just kept going. Giants All-Pro returner Dave Meggett appeared startled as the ball sailed over his head and rolled to the 6-yard line.

On the next play, defensive tackle Mike Golic sacked Phil Simms and caused a fumble that the Eagles recovered, and three plays later Keith Byars scored the game-winning touchdown on a two-yard run.

"That day, I told Buddy I could punt if he needed me," Cunningham said. "The wind was really swirling, but I knew if I got a hold of one, it would go. I was standing in

He wasn't a bad punter, but no one expected a kick booted by Randall Cunningham to travel 91 yards in a December 1989 game against the Giants in East Rutherford, New Jersey.

the back of the end zone. My foot was almost touching the end line. I knew I needed to hit it solid.

"Actually, I hit it a little off the end of my foot, but I got it off quickly, and it got up in the wind and it kept going. That wind made it hard to catch and Dave kind of misjudged it, I think. It got a good roll before he finally did pick it up. If he didn't get it to it, with the wind, it might have kept rolling, right through the tunnel onto the Jersey Turnpike."

Giants head coach Bill Parcells wasn't happy with his star returner.

"It's his job to catch the ball," Parcells said after the game. "He was three yards away. He should have attempted to catch it. I spent all day Saturday talking about that very situation, and I specifically mentioned that very situation."

Parcells continued to talk about Cunningham's punt for years to come as well.

"The night before [the game], Bill talked about it over and over—'hidden yards,' he called it—don't give up extra yards on a punt," said record-setting punter and future Eagle Sean Landeta, who had uncorked a then-career-long 71-yard punt moments earlier. "He brought that play up again in following years. Let's just say he wasn't real happy with David."

The Eagles were thrilled with Cunningham, who a year earlier had beaten the Giants with an incredible touch-

After backup punter Max Runager showed signs of struggle, Eagles head coach Buddy Ryan made the call to put Cunningham in for the kick.

Sean Landeta

One of the the longest punts ever by one of the NFL's greatest punters wasn't even the longest punt of the day. On the same day Eagles quarterback Randall Cunningham launched a 91-yard punt against the Giants, third-longest in NFL history, Sean Landeta of the Giants got off a 71-yarder of his own.

"It was one of the three coldest days I can remember," Landeta said of that November game at Giants Stadium. "The wind chill was minus 13. I punted from the same end zone Randall did about 10 minutes earlier. Mine went about 50 yards in the air, his went about 59. Mine bounced and took a hard shot to the left and went out of bounds for a 71-yarder.

"If it just took a different bounce, it would have gone about 90 yards, too. Imagine that. You could have had two 90-yard punts in the same game."

And you could have had two of the game's greatest punters.

Cunningham, one of the most exciting quarterbacks in NFL history, punted only 20 times in his 16-year career but averaged 44.7 yards.

Landeta, the NFL's All-Decade punter in both the 1980s and the 1990s, punted 1,401 times for a 43.3 average in his record-setting, 25-year pro career.

"I think of myself as both a Giant and an Eagle," Landeta says now. "I went to two Super Bowls with the Giants and two Pro Bowls. But I really enjoyed my four years in Philadelphia. I played on some great teams there with some great players."

down pass during which he bounced off Carl Banks. Now, he found another way to beat the Giants.

"In college he was one of the best punters in the country," Landeta said. "If he would have just concentrated on punting, he would have been terrific, probably one of the best who ever punted."

Cunningham wonders what might have been.

"People would tell me all the time to punt, but back then I didn't even think about it seriously," he said. "I didn't want to have to go out early to special teams practice and do all of that. I had enough to do as it was.

"Looking back, though, it would have been nice. I probably could have done it, and after going to Minnesota, to punt in a dome? Who knows what I might have done."

> **D**ave went back and got it, or it might have been 97 yards.
>
> —GIANTS PUNTER SEAN LANDETA

Game Details

Philadelphia Eagles 24 • New York Giants 17

Eagles	14	3	0	7	**24**
Giants	7	0	10	0	**17**

Date: December 3, 1989

Team Records: Philadelphia 8–4, New York 9–3

Scoring Plays:

PHI—Waters 3-yard fumble return (Ruzek PAT)

PHI—Simmons 60-yard interception return (Ruzek PAT)

NYG—Ingram 41-yard pass from Simms (Nittmo PAT)

PHI—Ruzek 35-yard FG

NYG—Nittmo 38-yard FG

NYG—Anderson 1-yard run (Nittmo PAT)

PHI—Byars 2-yard run (Ruzek PAT)

II

November 3, 1996

A Pick and a Pitch

Willis, Vincent Combine on Longest Interception Return in NFL History, 104 Yards to Beat Cowboys

James Willis knows what he should have done. And if he forgets, his players remind him. Willis, an Eagles linebacker in the mid-1990s and now a defensive coach at the University of Alabama, picked off a Troy Aikman pass four yards deep in the end zone with less than a minute to play to preserve a win over the Dallas Cowboys in 1996. What he did next, while going against conventional wisdom, led to one of the greatest plays in Eagles history.

"I should have just taken a knee in the end zone," Willis said. "I try to tell the kids I coach now to do that, and they say, 'Coach, you didn't do that in Dallas.' But I should have. I just saw all that open field in front of me and took off. Then I saw Troy [Vincent] and pitched it to him, and the rest is history."

Willis intercepted Aikman, ran out to the 10-yard line, and lateraled behind him to Vincent, who raced untouched the rest of the way for a touchdown, a 31–21 win, a 104-yard return, and, at the time, the longest interception return in NFL history.

"When it happened, I looked over and nobody was there," Vincent said. "Everyone was to the left and it was just [Willis] and me. He ran it out, and it became obvious he wasn't going to make it the whole way. I remember yelling, 'Will, I'm in back of you, I'm in back of you.' He tossed it over to me and I had the whole sideline in front of me."

James Willis makes for open field after intercepting Troy Aikman's pass intended for Tyji Armstrong (81) during the fourth quarter in Irving, Texas on November 3, 1996. Willis started a 104-yard play that ended with an Eagles touchdown and 31–21 victory over the Cowboys.

The Eagles, who had lost six straight games at Texas Stadium, including a 30–11 playoff loss the year before, had taken a 24–21 lead on Gary Anderson's 30-yard field goal with 3:19 to play. But Dallas, who had won three Super Bowls in the last four years with Aikman, Michael Irvin, and Emmitt Smith, came right back, as they always seemed to. Aikman completed two long passes, one to Irvin and one to Kelvin Martin, and the Cowboys drove down to the 3-yard line in the game's final moments and were primed to take the lead.

"I'm on the sidelines thinking, *Oh no, here we go again*," cornerback Bobby Taylor said. "I thought we were done."

On first-and-goal, Dallas ran its signature play, Smith on a sweep to the left, a play Smith used to score a majority of his 164 career touchdowns. This time, Vincent met him and threw him out of bounds after a gain of one yard. On second-and-goal, Dallas sent Smith up the middle, where extra linebacker Sylvester Wright—who only played 22 NFL games—crashed through and knocked the game's all-time leading rusher backward for a one-yard loss.

"We thought they were going to play it safe [on third down] and settle for a field goal," Willis said. "But they wanted to win the game right there and went for the touchdown. Yeah, you kind of take that a little personal."

Aikman was looking for backup tight end Tyji Armstrong, who had caught just two passes that entire season.

"I should have never thrown the ball," Aikman says today. "The play was 'I Right Tight Two Hot 204 F Flat,' and the first thing we want to do is get the ball to the fullback in the flat. But another guy who generally got the ball there was the tight end. We had a guy who was new to the system and a defense that was ready for the play."

Willis credits the Eagles' defensive coaches, head coach Ray Rhodes, and coordinator Emmitt Thomas for letting him know what was coming.

"All week we practiced against different packages they had, especially in the red zone," Willis said. "When I saw the play-fake, I knew what the play was. It's all about recognition."

That win moved the Eagles to 7–2 and into a tie for first place in the NFC East. They went on to earn a wild-card playoff berth.

"We needed to win that game," Vincent said. "And when you play Dallas, you don't just want to win, you really want to beat them. To be able to beat Dallas in Dallas was always special, and that was right in the middle of their run. That was their era, with Troy and Emmitt and Michael.

"In the red zone, they were a machine. The plays they ran were automatic. We knew we had to man up and make a play. I think that was the start of things for our defense."

Game Details

Philadelphia Eagles 31 • Dallas Cowboys 21

Eagles	7	7	7	10	**31**
Cowboys	7	3	3	8	**21**

Date: November 3, 1996

Team Records: Philadelphia 6–4, Dallas 5–3

Scoring Plays:

DAL—Smith 1-yard run (Boniol PAT)

PHI—Watters 5-yard run (Anderson PAT)

DAL—Boniol 19-yard FG

PHI—Detmer 6-yard run (Anderson PAT)

DAL—Boniol 37-yard FG

PHI—Fryar 14-yard pass from Detmer (Anderson PAT)

DAL—Smith 7-yard run (Bjornson pass from Aikman)

PHI—Anderson 30-yard FG

PHI—Willis (14) and Vincent (90) 104-yard interception return

> **A**s soon as I let go of the ball, I knew it was trouble. The linebacker was there, and that was that.
>
> —TROY AIKMAN

Troy Vincent

When the Dolphins declined to match the Eagles' offer sheet for Troy Vincent, it was one of the best things that ever happened for Vincent. And for the Eagles. Vincent, who played football at Pennsbury High, 25 miles north of Broad and Pattison, made his homecoming a huge success, becoming one of the greatest cornerbacks in Eagles history.

"I had a ton of respect for Ray Rhodes from his days in San Francisco, and to be able to play for Emmitt Thomas, a Hall of Famer, it was a dream come true," Vincent said. "But for me to come home, I was taking a huge risk. You never know what could happen in that situation. But I believed in my ability, and I believed in the team. It turned out to be the best decision of my professional career."

Vincent is a member of the Eagles' all-time team, but his work off the field has been even more impressive. He became the first NFL player to win the Walter Payton Man of the Year Award, the Byron "Whizzer" White Award, the Bart Starr Award, and the *Sporting News*' No. 1 Good Guy Award.

In his eight years with the Eagles (1996–2003), Vincent had 28 interceptions and went to five Pro Bowls. In 1999, he became the first Eagle in 27 years to lead the NFL in interceptions.

"And what made it even better was we had success," Vincent said. "Not the ultimate success we wanted, but we had some really good years in Philly."

One of the greatest corners in Eagles history, Troy Vincent grew up in the Philadelphia area.

10

November 19, 1978

Miracle of the Meadowlands

Edwards TD Return of Fumbled Pisarcik Handoff to Csonka Shocks Giants

After the game ended, Bill Bergey got on the phone with Eagles owner Leonard Tose, who was 1,600 miles away in a Houston hospital, recovering from a medical procedure.

"I remember telling him, 'You're not going to believe how we won,'" Bergey says now. "I know I don't believe it.'"

It really was a miracle. All the Giants had to do to finish off a 17–12 win over the Eagles was run out the clock and have quarterback Joe Pisarcik take a knee on a couple snaps. But the play call from Giants offensive coordinator Bob Gibson was different. It wasn't a knee, it was Pro 65 Up, a handoff from Pisarcik to fullback Larry Csonka. Csonka gained 11 yards, and Gibson called the same play again.

"One of their linemen yelled out, 'Joe, just take a knee,'" Bergey said. "And Joe said, 'No, we better run the play they told us to run.'"

Pisarcik had changed a call at the line of scrimmage a week earlier in a loss to the Redskins and was yelled at by his coaches. He wasn't going to do it again.

"I felt it was a secure play," Giants head coach John McVay said after the game. "How [much more] secure

can you get [than] giving the ball to the fullback and running it?"

Only 31 seconds remained in the game. There was no way the Giants could lose.

"We knew it would take a miracle to win the game, but as long as there was time left on the clock, we were still going to play hard," Bergey said. "I told Frank [LeMaster], 'Let's both blitz in the same gap,' and we did."

Pisarcik pivoted and handed the ball to Csonka, who had been a five-time Pro Bowl pick with the Dolphins before joining the Giants late in his career. Csonka, who lined up in the wrong spot after complaining bitterly in the huddle about the play call, never secured the handoff, and the ball popped loose, ricocheting around Pisarcik's hands before hitting the ground. Eagles cornerback Herm Edwards, who was beat on a 30-yard touchdown pass earlier in the game from Pisarcik to Johnny Perkins, picked up the ball on one bounce and started running.

"Herm Edwards was playing eight to 10 yards deep, but he took two giants steps and then he was at the line of scrimmage," Bergey said. "Before anybody knew what happened, Herm picked the ball up."

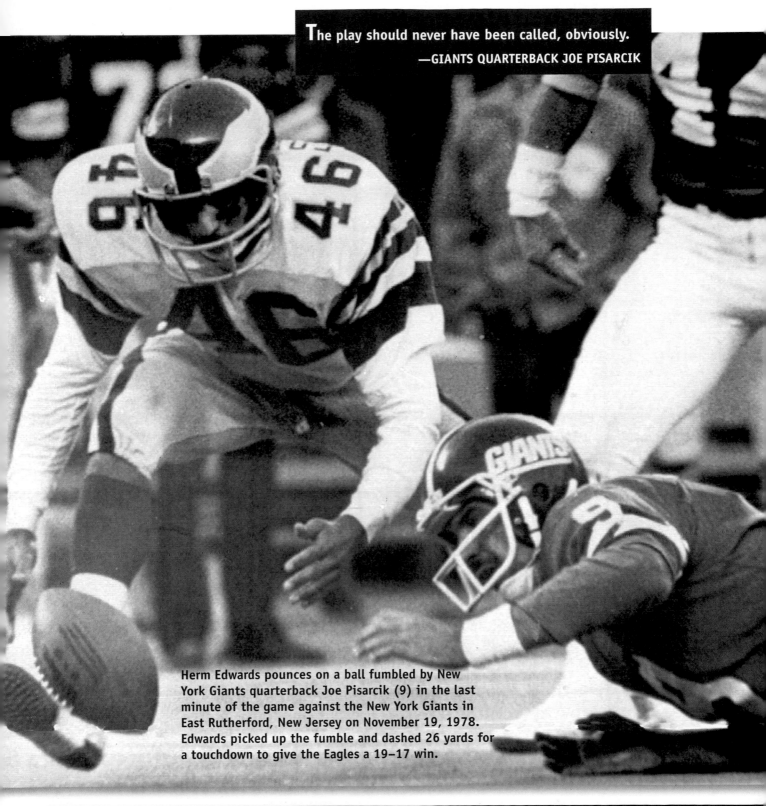

Herm Edwards pounces on a ball fumbled by New York Giants quarterback Joe Pisarcik (9) in the last minute of the game against the New York Giants in East Rutherford, New Jersey on November 19, 1978. Edwards picked up the fumble and dashed 26 yards for a touchdown to give the Eagles a 19–17 win.

Edwards, who would go on to become head coach of the New York Jets and the Kansas City Chiefs, was in his second NFL season. He didn't hesitate. He scooped up the ball on one hop and was off to the end zone before anybody realized what happened.

"I remember how silent the stadium got," said NFL historian Ray Didinger, who was on the sideline, covering the game for the old *Philadelphia Bulletin*. "You could actually hear Herm's feet as he ran toward the end zone. I could see the look in his eyes, too, and he was wide-eyed, almost in disbelief, just like everyone else."

Edwards ran 26 yards for a touchdown, and the legend of "the Miracle of the Meadowlands" was born.

"I was just stunned that something like that could happen," Eagles coach Dick Vermeil says now. "They were running out the clock, and next thing you know there's great jubilation on our sideline and everybody is jumping up and down celebrating. I looked over at the other side of the field and felt sorry for their coach."

Game Details

Philadelphia Eagles 19 • New York Giants 17

Eagles	0	6	0	13	**19**
Giants	14	0	3	0	**17**

Date: November 19, 1978

Team Records: Philadelphia 6–5, New York 5–6

Scoring Plays:

NYG—Hammond 19-yard pass from Pisarcik (Danelo PAT)

NYG—Perkins 30-yard pass from Pisarcik (Danelo PAT)

PHI—Montgomery 8-yard run (kick failed)

NYG—Danelo 37-yard FG

PHI—Hogan 1-yard run

PHI—Edwards 26-yard fumble return (Michel PAT)

Herm Edwards scores the winning touchdown with 20 seconds left in the game after recovering Joe Pisarcik's fumble.

Edwards scored untouched. He was 10 yards down the field before any Giants realized he had the ball. Backup tight end Gary Shirk tried to pursue Edwards but never got close to him.

"I really didn't know what happened," Edwards said. "All I saw was the ball. I wanted to make something happen, too. I owed the team one. I blew the coverage on the touchdown and, deep down inside, I thought, *Hey, I've got to make a play.*"

The Eagles won 19–17, and thanks to that miracle they finished 9–7 and made the playoffs for the first time in 18 years. Gibson was fired the next day.

"I've been in this game 25 years," McVay said. "And that's the most horrifying end to a game I've ever seen."

Phil Tuckett

Phil Tuckett could have packed up and left. He could have gone home. He could have done anything other than shooting the final meaningless plays of an unremarkable NFL game.

Tuckett, who had played briefly for the San Diego Chargers in 1968, was a 32-year-old cameraman for NFL Films in the fall of 1978, and his assignment on November 19 was to shoot the Eagles-Giants game at the Meadowlands. The entire game.

So with the Giants leading 17–12 and running out the clock, Tuckett moved to the west end zone.

"I reveled in the nuances and the details that made this a unique event, so I started shooting with the warm-ups and kept going until the teams went down the tunnel after the game," Tuckett says today.

"Sometimes you don't know what a particular game's storyline is going to be until the end of the game or even after the game. Was it two players talking? Players on the bench reacting to a devastating defeat? It wasn't a matter of thinking, *Oh, the game is over. I can pack up now.* I didn't look at it that way."

Good thing, too, because that legendary footage of Eagles cornerback Herm Edwards running into the end zone scoring the winning touchdown in one of the most celebrated games in NFL history exists because of it.

"The ball popped out, and it was weird—since I was always prepared in case something like that ever happened, I wasn't even surprised," Tuckett said. "It was like I had seen the play before. The ball immediately went up in the air, but it stayed in my frame, which was good for me, because I didn't have to hunt for it rolling around on the ground. Herm picked up the ball and never broke stride. The strange thing was, he could have taken any route to the end zone—there was nobody near him—but he made a slight turn, right toward me."

There was no network camera in the end zone back then. Nobody in the stands was filming with a cell phone. There was only Tuckett, recording every historic moment of the Miracle of the Meadowlands on Kodak 16-millimeter color reversal film through a 30-pound German Aeroflex camera.

"The next day, [NFL Films founder] Ed Sabol came into my office and hugged me," Tuckett said. "He said, 'That was the perfect football shot.'"

Tuckett went on to become an NFL Films vice president, won 28 Emmy Awards, filmed music videos for Aerosmith, Santana, and Metallica, and even won a Billboard Music Award. In 2007, disillusioned with NFL Films' direction ("more quantity, less quality"), he returned to his alma mater, Dixie College in St. George, Utah, to teach digital film production.

"There are so many variables shooting football that it's almost impossible to ever get a perfect document of a play," Tuckett said. "I just happened to get a perfect document of that one. And it just happened to be one of the greatest plays in NFL history."

November 10, 1985

99 Yards in Overtime

Jaworski, Quick Connect on Record-Setting Pass

The Eagles had blown all of a 17-point fourth-quarter lead and now found themselves in overtime against an Atlanta Falcons team that was sputtering along at 1–8. Atlanta's Rick Donnelly, punting from his 37-yard line, got off a beauty. The ball sailed high and deep. It landed at the Eagles' 10, took a good bounce, and rolled out of bounds at the 1-yard line.

The Eagles were in trouble. On their first offensive play of overtime, the Eagles tried to go for it all, but quarterback Ron Jaworski misfired on a deep ball for second-year wide receiver Kenny Jackson. All the momentum was with the Falcons.

"We didn't get anything on first down and now we're in the huddle and we were saying, 'Let's just get some yards, let's run a quick hitch or something.' We needed to get out of the end zone and just get some breathing room," Pro Bowl wide receiver Mike Quick remembered.

The Eagles got more than that. Quick did run a hitch, and Jaworski hit him in stride just short of the 20-yard line. Nearly 80 yards later, they had matched a record that will never be broken for longest offensive play in NFL history.

"We knew if we could get the corner to play outside, Mike would have a chance to split the zone," Jaworski said. "That's exactly what he did. He split the zone, and he was gone."

Quick saw the same thing his quarterback did, and he turned it into history.

Quarterback Ron Jaworski knew if he could get the ball to wideout Mike Quick, the speedy receiver could split the zone in a November 1985 game against the Atlanta Falcons.

Mike Quick

From 1983 through 1987, Mike Quick was one of the NFL's best players on one of its worst teams. When the Eagles got good, Quick got hurt.

"That's the shame of it," Eagles linebacker Garry Cobb said. "He missed his chance for true greatness. As bad as some of those Eagles teams were, Quick was still one of the marquee receivers of his era. But could you imagine if he was on a better team? He was making great plays, but nobody outside of Philly really knew. If he would have stayed healthy a few more years, he would be in the Hall of Fame."

During those five seasons, Quick made five straight Pro Bowls and caught 309 passes for 5,437 yards and 53 touchdowns. But after injuries limited him to just 18 games on playoff-bound teams in the next three years, he retired.

"Timing is everything," Quick said. "Fortunately, I was in the right place at the right time to make it to the NFL. But I caught Ron [Jaworski] at the end of his career and Randall [Cunningham] when he was still green."

Quick played in just one postseason game, the Fog Bowl loss to the Bears in 1988.

"The guy was unbelievable," teammate Eric Allen said. "He was uncoverable. He was a little bit more physical than [Randy] Moss, a little bigger than Marvin Harrison, and you couldn't jam him because he was so quick. If he stayed healthy? I can't even imagine the numbers he would have put up."

Eagles receiver Mike Quick is one of the greatest wide receivers in Eagles history but only played in one postseason game—a loss to the Bears in the Fog Bowl on New Year's Eve 1988.

"When I lined up, the cornerback, Bobby Butler, was shading me outside," Quick said. "The safety, Scott Case, he was at the hash marks. Where he was, you couldn't tell if they were in a Cover 2 or a Cover 3. On the snap, the cornerback started to backpedal, so it looked like Cover 3.

"I caught the ball [and] glanced at the safety just to see where he was. I wasn't worried about the cornerback at that point, because I knew I was by him. Case was coming at me, but he didn't have the angle. So I turned upfield, started running, and lo and behold, I was in the end zone."

The 23–17 win evened the Eagles' record at 5–5 and gave the franchise its first-ever overtime victory.

"We went into that overtime a little shaky," linebacker Garry Cobb said. "We felt we had blown the game. The defense was reeling a little bit. We stopped them on the drive, and then we barely got off the field and we look up and there's Quick going all the way."

Quick knew how to get in the end zone. From 1983 through 1987, he scored an NFL-best 53 touchdowns. Besides the record-setting 99-yarder, he also had long TD catches of 90, 83, 82, and 75 yards.

"I remember when I got to Philly everyone told me how great Mike Quick was and how he can make big plays for you," said Randall Cunningham, who was a rookie backup that year. "That was about as big of a play as you can make."

It was the kind that great receivers make, turning a play designed to get a first down into a huge touchdown.

"Mike's speed was always deceptive," Cobb said. "He gets faster as he starts running. Once he gets into stride, he's gone. He never looked as fast as he was, because he was so smooth."

Even so, that play isn't Quick's favorite. "My favorite play was another game against Atlanta, in

Game Details

Philadelphia Eagles 23 • Atlanta Falcons 17 (OT)

Eagles	0	14	3	0	6	**23**
Falcons	0	0	0	17	0	**17**

Date: November 10, 1985

Team Records: Philadelphia 4–5, Atlanta 1–8

Scoring Plays:

PHI—Jackson 8-yard run (McFadden PAT)

PHI—Jaworski 1-yard run (McFadden PAT)

PHI—McFadden 30-yard FG

ATL—Washington 18-yard pass from Archer (Luckhurst PAT)

ATL—Riggs 1-yard run (Luckhurst PAT)

ATL—Luckhurst 27-yard FG

PHI—Quick 99-yard pass from Jaworski

Atlanta," he said. "I was pretty well covered, but Ron threw me open. He put it in the corner of the end zone and I stretched out parallel to the ground in the air and made a one-handed catch with my left hand. It stuck and I pulled it in."

The 99-yarder remains the most memorable.

"As I was running, it was like, 'This isn't actually happening,'" Quick said. "It was the kind of stuff you dream about."

> **I** just hit it, and I knew they couldn't catch me. I just ran until I got to the end zone.
>
> **—MIKE QUICK**

8

October 19, 2003

Season-Saving Return

Westbrook's 84-yard Punt Return Steals Win over Giants, Sparks Winning Streak

The game was over. The season was over. Sure, the Eagles would get the ball back deep in their own territory with about a minute to play. But they had managed only 135 yards in the game, just 24 after halftime. They were about to lose their second consecutive division game and fall to 2–4, three games behind the surging Cowboys. They looked dead.

And then a punt bounced into Brian Westbrook's hands.

"It's one of my most memorable plays, mainly because of the magnitude it had in the game," Westbrook said. "If it happened in the first quarter, it wouldn't be the same. When it happened and how it happened just magnified it."

The Giants, leading 10–7 with 1:34 left, could have clinched a win with a first down, but the Eagles forced a punt and Jeff Feagles, one of the best ever, kicked from just inside midfield.

"Feagles is a great right-sideline punter," said John Harbaugh, then the Eagles' special teams coach, now head coach of the Ravens. "He'll put the ball out of bounds 45 yards down the field 98 times out of 100."

This time, thanks to a heavy Eagles rush from Feagles' right, Sheldon Brown in particular, he was forced to kick the ball in play.

"We wanted to get as much pressure as possible so he'd have to rush that kick and bring the ball up the middle a little more," Harbaugh said. "And that's exactly what happened."

Westbrook fielded the ball at the 16-yard line on one big bounce, picked up a block from Pro Bowl special-teamer Ike Reese, turned down the left sideline, and 84 yards later gave the Eagles a 14–10 lead over the stunned Giants.

"We really couldn't get anything going on offense," Westbrook said. "Now it was the end of the game, and they had to punt. I was just hoping for a returnable punt, to get an opportunity to do something. The last thing I wanted was for it to keep bouncing and us having to go 98 yards or something like that."

Giants receiver David Tyree raced down the field toward Westbrook, a step ahead of Reese. When the ball bounced, Tyree slowed down to see what Westbrook would do. That gave Reese a chance to get in front of him enough to slow him down. The Giants felt Reese's block was illegal. It was very close.

"I gave him a little box-out block, just a nudge," Reese said. "Then I fell over and gave the old 'I'm innocent' look to make sure there wasn't a flag."

By letting the ball bounce, Westbrook gave Reese time to disrupt Tyree enough to take him out of the play.

"If he runs up and tries to catch it, he'll get blasted because there's a guy who's running down the field who isn't blocked," Reese said. "He's going to get killed. So Westbrook had enough confidence that I was going to get there that he let it bounce because he didn't want to run up and catch the ball and have a collision. [Then] it's a fumble, it's a muffed punt. He took the safe route by letting it bounce, which gave me a chance to get down there."

And it gave the Giants a false sense of security.

"I knew once the ball hit the ground we were in trouble," Giants running back Tiki Barber says now. "I used to be a punt returner, and I know that when a ball hits the ground, everybody kind of takes a deep breath and relaxes because you don't think there's going to be a return. If he caught it in the air, we would have been fine. When he picked it up on a bounce, I knew he was gone."

Once Westbrook eluded Tyree, the Giants had no shot. "I got out, made a couple of guys miss, and headed down the sideline," Westbrook said.

Westbrook scored with 76 seconds left. The Giants challenged the play, claiming Westbrook stepped out of bounds. They lost.

"I watched the whole play from the ground thinking, *Thank goodness I didn't blow this play by getting a block in the back*," Reese said.

Brian Westbrook celebrates as he crosses the goal line with the game-winning 84-yard punt return for a touchdown against the New York Giants on October 19, 2003 in East Rutherford, New Jersey.

Westbrook soars for a touchdown during the NFC divisional playoff game at the Louisiana Superdome against the Saints in New Orleans on January 13, 2007.

Brian Westbrook

When Eagles scouting director Marc Ross first saw Brian Westbrook, he laughed. Three years later, he knew the Eagles had to have him.

"I went to see him as a freshman and said, 'Are you kidding me?'" Ross said. "He didn't look like a NFL player."

Yet the Eagles kept an eye on Westbrook, and by the time he was done rewriting the Division 1-AA record books at Villanova, they knew he was their guy.

"I'd love to be able to tell you I knew, or we knew, how good he would be," Ross said. "The truth is, he kept getting better."

The Eagles were hoping for another Dave Meggett. Instead, they got another Marshall Faulk.

"I was always being doubted because I wasn't big enough or I didn't go to a big enough school," Westbrook said. "I just wanted a chance."

Westbrook went to his first Pro Bowl in 2004 and led the NFL with 2,104 total yards in 2007, when he

> **W**e weren't having our best season. We needed something to spark us, get us going, and I guess that did it.
>
> —EAGLES PUNT RETURNER BRIAN WESTBROOK

broke the franchise record held by Wilbert Montgomery. By 2008, he ranked third in team history in catches, rushing yards and TDs.

"I scouted Brian at Villanova when I was [coaching] with the Rams," Montgomery said. "I wrote in my report, 'Brian Westbrook is the Marshall Faulk of college football'—and I saved it just in case people didn't believe me. What he's able to do is unbelievable. People looked at Brian Westbrook's stature and said, 'He can't do this, he can't do that.' But you can't measure a man's heart."

The Eagles had a 14–10 win, the first of nine consecutive wins that led to a 12–4 record, an NFC East title, and a third-straight trip to the NFC Championship Game.

"I remember their tight end, [Visanthe] Shiancoe, had an angle on Brian," Harbaugh said. "I was thinking, *OK, we're getting a good return, at least the offense will have a chance.* But Brian just blew by him, and that was the first time I really saw just how legitimately fast he was. He found a gear I didn't know he had."

That extra gear eventually helped Westbrook become a Pro Bowl tailback. But it was that scintillating punt return that put him on the map.

"I was still trying to find myself, really," Westbrook said. "But that play, the return, catapulted my career. People started noticing me more after that."

Game Details

Philadelphia Eagles 14 • New York Giants 10

Eagles	7	0	0	7	**14**
Giants	0	3	7	0	**10**

Date: October 19, 2003

Team Records: Philadelphia 2–3, New York 2–3

Scoring Plays:

PHI—Westbrook 6-yard run (Akers PAT)

NYG—Conway 39-yard FG

NYG—Shockey 1-yard pass from Collins (Conway PAT)

PHI—Westbrook 84-yard punt return (Akers PAT)

December 2, 1990

"Sometimes, I Amaze Myself"

Cunningham Eludes Bruce Smith, Avoids Safety, Throws 95-Yard Strike to Barnett for Second-Longest Touchdown Pass in Eagles History

Randall Cunningham's quote gained almost as much notoriety as the play itself. Cunningham had turned in one of the most remarkable plays of his 16-year career earlier in the day, escaping a certain safety at the hands of Bruce Smith to deliver a 95-yard miracle to Freddie Barnett. The Bills had won 30–23, but much of the focus in his post-game press conference was on the 95-yard touchdown, the second-longest TD pass in Eagles history.

"Do you ever amaze yourself?" Cunningham was asked as he stood at a podium near the visiting locker room at Rich Stadium.

The quarterback, known for his honesty off the field as much as his playmaking abilities on it, answered the only way he knew how.

"Yes," he said, "sometimes I even amaze myself."

He wasn't being cocky. He wasn't bragging. He was just answering the question. But it infuriated a fan base who felt it was inappropriate for Cunningham to say after a loss.

"The question was asked about that play, 'Do you amaze yourself?'" Cunningham says today. "What am I supposed to say? Of course I amaze myself when I create a play that people think is an amazing play. It's not like I planned to do those things. It's by instinct. Then people say, 'Oh, he has an ego problem.' If I had said, 'No, I don't amaze myself, I expect to do that,' they would say he's the cockiest person ever. So you really can't win."

The Bills took an early 24–0 lead, still the third-most points the Eagles have ever allowed in a first quarter. Late in the second quarter, they still trailed 24–9 and were backed up at their 5-yard line facing third-and-14.

"Buffalo jumped on us early that day," Cunningham said. "We needed to make something happen, and we were back near our goal line."

Then the unbelievable happened.

"Calvin [Williams] was the primary receiver on the play," Barnett said. "He ran a square route, and I ran

Randall Cunningham was one of the first multi-threat quarterbacks who could beat teams with his arm or legs. In an epic play against the Bills in December 1990, he did both.

a post to try and clear out the middle for him. Buffalo's defense was so good then. They had Bruce Smith, Cornelius Bennett, Darryl Talley, and I'm sure I'm forgetting some guys. We had struggled against them all game."

Cunningham took the snap from center with 1:10 on the clock and didn't uncork his throw to Barnett until there was 1:02 left. In those eight seconds, he avoided a sack from Smith, who finished his Hall of Fame career with more sacks than anybody in history, and danced away from two other Bills.

"I'm just trying to make a play, and I'm saying to myself, *I can't take a safety here. I just can't take a safety*," Cunningham said. "I knew Bruce was coming, and I knew Cornelius Bennett was coming on the other side.

"The crowd was pretty loud, and it was definitely hard to hear. I kept going back, and almost stepped out of the end zone. I tried to spin back and that's when he was closing in on me. I caught Bruce out of the corner of my right eye and just ducked under him."

Then he saw Barnett, the rookie third-round pick from Arkansas State, who was playing in his 12th NFL game.

"I'm about 25, 30 yards downfield and I look back, and I just see bodies flying around," Barnett recalled. "I'm standing there, and I'm not sure what's going on, because I really can't tell. All I see is all kinds of action back near the end zone. Then I see Randall run to his left, my right, and he comes out of a pile. He sets and he points. We had gone over this a million times. When he points to me, he's going to throw it up for me. So I take off, and he lets it go."

Cunningham knew Barnett was athletic enough to make a play when there wasn't one there to make.

"Fred was out there, and I knew he could jump because he high jumped seven feet once in high school," Cunningham said. "I threw it out there and hoped he would go up and get it. And that's what he did."

Barnett caught the ball at the Bills' 40-yard line. The rest was easy.

"The ball had a lot of height on it," Barnett said. "The cornerback, James Williams, who was covering me, jumped too soon. He misjudged it and then fell. I caught it and started running to the end zone. There wasn't anyone near me, but I still ran like I was being chased."

Game Details

Buffalo Bills 30 • Philadelphia Eagles 23

Bills	24	0	3	3	**30**
Eagles	0	16	7	0	**23**

Date: December 2, 1990

Team Records: Philadelphia 7–4, Buffalo 9–2

Scoring Plays:

BUF—Lofton 63-pass from Kelly (Norwood PAT)

BUF—Norwood 43-yard FG

BUF—Reed 56-pass from Kelly (Norwood PAT)

BUF—Thomas 4-pass from Kelly (Norwood PAT)

PHI—Jackson 18-pass from Cunningham (kick failed)

PHI—Ruzek 32-yard FG

PHI—Barnett 95-pass from Cunningham (Ruzek PAT)

PHI—Byars 1-yard run (Ruzek PAT)

BUF—Norwood 21-yard FG

BUF—Norwood 45-yard FG

> **R**andall was a playmaker. I used to tell him go out and make plays, and we'll win the game. We didn't win that one, but he made the play.
>
> —BUDDY RYAN

Rookie Wideouts

Ron Johnson and Gregg Garrity were journeymen. Mike Quick's brilliant career was coming to an end. Cris Carter was in and out of drug rehab. It wasn't hard to figure out where the Eagles would go in the 1990 draft.

"We needed receivers, a bunch of 'em," head coach Buddy Ryan recalled. "There wasn't one who jumped out at me in the first round, so I took the corner from Georgia [Ben Smith]. Then we just started taking receivers."

Ryan picked Mike Bellamy of Illinois in the second round, Fred Barnett of Arkansas State in the third round, and Purdue's Calvin Williams in the fifth round. Bellamy played just six NFL games and didn't catch a pass. But Barnett and Williams became two of the top receivers in Eagles history.

"Buddy never really treated us as rookies," Barnett said. "He told us right from the start the best players were going to play. It was a great opportunity for us. Buddy used to say, 'Catch the ball or you're fired.'"

Williams caught nine touchdowns in 1990 and Barnett eight, still the top rookie performances in franchise history. Going into 2009, both still ranked among the top 10 in Eagles history in catches, yards, and touchdowns.

"You look back and say, 'Wow,' but at the time it didn't seem like a big deal," Williams said. "We had such a good supporting cast with Keith Jackson at tight end and Keith Byars coming out of the backfield. There wasn't a real lot asked of us."

Fred Barnett makes a nice one-handed grab during a game against the Washington Redskins on October 8, 1995 at Veterans Stadium in Philadelphia.

6

December 19, 1948

Steve Van Buren 7, Chicago Cardinals 0

Van Buren Scores Only TD in 1948 Title Game After Blizzard Nearly Keeps Him Home

The journey to the game took all morning. The journey to the end zone took all afternoon.

December 19, 1948, began with a titanic blizzard sweeping through Philadelphia and ended with the first NFL Championship in franchise history. And Steve Van Buren was in the middle of all of it.

In 1948, Van Buren was the best football player in the world, and on December 19, he would get his chance to carry the Eagles to their first NFL title, against the Chicago Cardinals at Shibe Park. But when Van Buren looked outside his home in Haverford, Pennsylvania, he saw so much snow he assumed the game would be postponed.

"Most of the players had arrived at Shibe Park, and they looked around and realized Steve wasn't there yet," NFL historian Ray Didinger said. "People were starting to get a little concerned."

So coach Greasy Neale called Van Buren to make sure he knew the game was still on.

"Greasy said, 'Hey listen, we are going to play today, I would suggest you get going,'" Didinger said.

If Neale hadn't made that call, who knows? Needless to say, things might have turned out a little differently. As it was, Van Buren's car was buried in so

Steve Van Buren (15) plunges over the goal line with a fourth quarter touchdown that defeated the Chicago Cardinals in the driving snowstorm in Philadelphia on December 19, 1948.

Steve Van Buren poses for an undated hero shot during his career with the Eagles.

much snow he couldn't drive. So he found another way to get to Shibe Park.

It's hard to imagine today, but that morning, one of the greatest players in NFL history rode a bus to 69th Street, then jumped on the Market-Frankford El to City Hall, then transferred to the Broad Street subway, which he took to Lehigh Avenue. Then he walked six long blocks west along snow-covered streets to Shibe Park, which sat at Lehigh and 20th.

"That was the National Football League in 1948," Didinger said.

When Van Buren finally arrived, he found a field buried under so much snow that stadium workers couldn't remove the tarp. So players from both teams were recruited to the grounds crew, and the game was delayed 30 minutes. But the snow continued falling, making conditions virtually impossible. Nobody could see yard lines or the sidelines or even be sure where the end zone was—not that it mattered for most of the game, because nobody got near it.

"I was starting to think nobody's going to score," Wistert recalls today. "I thought, *We're going to be out here all night.*"

There was no score late in the third quarter when Chicago's Elmer Angsman, who had scored two 70-yard touchdowns a year earlier in the Cards' 28–21 win over the Eagles in the 1947 NFL Championship Game, fumbled a handoff and Bucko Kilroy recovered the ball at the Cardinals' 17-yard line. Four plays later, on the second play of

The 1947 Game

The Packers are the only franchise in history to win three straight NFL championships. In the 1940s, the Eagles nearly added their name to that exclusive list.

In 1947, a year before they won the first of two consecutive NFL titles, the Eagles lost to the Cardinals, 28–21, in the NFL Championship Game in Chicago.

"We should have had three in a row," All-Pro lineman Al Wistert said in the winter of 2009, soon after he turned 88. "The one we lost in 1947, we should have won that one."

The day before the game, the Eagles practiced along the sidelines at Comiskey, since the field was covered.

"When we were leaving, we saw the grounds crew taking the tarp off the field," Wistert said. "We told the guy in charge, 'You have to do that tomorrow,' and he said, 'We can't, because then we'll have to pay them time and a half.' That was their excuse for taking the tarp off the field on Saturday."

Wistert knew a frozen field meant doom for Hall of Fame running back Steve Van Buren. And the next day, Van Buren, the greatest running back of his generation, ran 18 times for just 26 yards.

"It was impossible to get your footing, the field was so frozen," Wistert said. "Steve was the best back in the league, but on that field, he couldn't do anything. If they kept that field covered until Sunday, we would have won that game, and we would have won three straight championships."

the fourth quarter, the Eagles found themselves five yards from the end zone.

Everybody knew who would get the ball. Van Buren lined up to the left of fullback Joe Muha in the backfield, took the handoff from quarterback Tommy Thompson moving to the right, then immediately cut left and into the end zone behind blocks from Muha and Wistert.

"Steve just ran right behind me," Wistert says. "Nobody even touched him."

That touchdown gave the Eagles a 7–0 win in the lowest-scoring championship game in NFL history. The 1948 and 1949 Eagles remain the only team to win consecutive NFL championship games by shutout.

"We wanted that shutout," Wistert said. "We had an agreement with Old Bookbinders down at 2nd and Walnut that if we ever had a shutout, the whole team was invited to dinner. Players, wives, children—everybody. Old Bookbinders was a wonderful eating house and we wanted to have a meal down there. That was on our minds that whole game."

Game Details

Philadelphia Eagles 7 • Chicago Cardinals 0

Eagles	0	0	0	7	**7**
Cardinals	0	0	0	0	**0**

Date: December 19, 1948
Team Records: Philadelphia 9–2–1, Chicago 11–1
Scoring Plays:
PHI—Van Buren 5-yard run (Patton PAT)

He looked out the window and thought he'd go back to bed. Fortunately, he didn't.

—EAGLES LINEMAN AL WISTERT

5

October 3, 1993

"The Greatest Interception Return in NFL History"

Allen Hands Ball to Injured Cunningham After Spectacular 94-Yard Interception Return Against Jets

The only thing more dramatic than the interception return itself was what happened after it. When Eric Allen intercepted quarterback Boomer Esiason in the fourth quarter of an Eagles-Jets game in 1993, he didn't see any reason to try a return. There was no clear path down the field, no apparent route to pick up yardage.

"I was going to just run out of bounds," Allen says now.

The Jets led 30–28 and had possession deep in Eagles territory. It had already been a brutal day for the 3–0 Eagles, who lost franchise quarterback Randall Cunningham, Pro Bowl receiver Fred Barnett, and returner Jeff Sydner to season-ending knee injuries. And now the Jets were about to take a two-possession lead.

Defensive tackle Keith Millard had blasted Esiason with a late hit a moment earlier, and

though the penalty gave the Jets 15 yards, it was worth it. Esiason was still shaken up. On second down, Esiason spotted Chris Burkett near the left sideline and threw as Millard arrived again. Allen, already one of the NFL's finest cornerbacks in just his third season, flew in front of Burkett and picked off Esiason at the 6-yard line.

"I wasn't thinking about a big return, but I began to see some of their offensive linemen walking toward the sideline," Allen said. "There's no interest in me. So now I'm thinking, *OK, I'm going to get as many yards as I can.* But I still wasn't thinking about going all the way. I went back to Pop Warner—there's an opening here, an opening there. If a guy was bigger than me, I ran around him, and if there was a guy smaller than me, I ran through him."

Allen caught the ball near the Jets' sideline, eluded a few would-be tacklers with a spin move he picked up as a kid watching Redskins running

Eric Allen was known for his interceptions—and subsequent returns—including one of the most spectacular in NFL lore.

back Larry Brown, ran up the middle through traffic, then made his way to the opposite side of the field and broke down the Eagles' sideline into the end zone.

"It seemed like every hole I ran through was about to close, but I got through it just before it did," Allen said. "Then I picked up some blocks and started going. I remember Ben Smith running in front of me and yelling for me to pitch it to him. Pitch it? Are you kidding me?"

No, this play belonged to Allen.

"He was zig-zagging all over the place," defensive tackle Andy Harmon said. "You wanted to block somebody, but you didn't know which way to block because you didn't know which way he was going next."

By the time Allen crossed the goal line, he had covered about 150 yards in what was officially a 94-yard return. The Eagles won 35–30, and Allen had produced what Steve Sabol of NFL Films called the greatest interception return in NFL history.

"It's an heirloom to be passed down from generation to generation," Sabol said.

Allen's play was already historic. What happened next made it legendary. Cunningham, who had just learned his season was over, was watching the game from inside the tunnel on the west side of Giants Stadium.

"I was standing in the tunnel," Cunningham recalled. "I just saw the X-ray on my leg and was feeling down. I needed surgery and I knew my season was over. Then I heard Fred and Jeff Sydner got hurt, too. It was a bad day. Then Eric made that play. It was an incredible run. I wanted to jump up and down, but then I remembered I was on crutches."

As it happened, Allen's return brought him into that same end zone. Without pausing, Allen handed Cunningham the ball.

"That meant so much to me," Cunningham said. "It was just a great feeling after feeling so bad before that. I mean, you're standing there hopeless, helpless—and then he gives you the game ball."

It was a simple gesture loaded with symbolism. Earlier in the day, the ball had been taken away from Cunningham. Allen gave it back.

"We were such a close team and it hit me right then that his season was over," Allen said. "After all the ups and downs of the season, him getting hurt for the second time in three years, after all he'd been through, Reggie [White] had left. Randall was our leader and his season was over, and I wanted to make sure he realized and that everybody recognized what a big part of our team he still was. I wanted him to feel, 'Hey, you're not by yourself. You're still a big part of this team.'"

> **H**e ran about 200 yards to go about 90 yards.
> —EAGLES LINEBACKER SETH JOYNER

Game Details

Philadelphia Eagles 35 • New York Jets 30

Eagles	0	14	7	14	**35**
Jets	14	7	7	2	**30**

Date: October 3, 1993
Team Records: Philadelphia 3–0, New York 2–1
Scoring Plays:

NYJ—Thornton 7-yard pass from Esiason (Blanchard PAT)
NYJ—Mitchell 14-yard pass from Esiason (Blanchard PAT)
NYJ—Mitchell 12-yard pass from Esiason (Blanchard PAT)
PHI—Walker 8-yard run (Bahr PAT)
PHI—Bavaro 10-yard pass from Brister (Bahr PAT)
NYJ—Mitchell 65-yard pass from Esiason (Blanchard PAT)
PHI—Williams 11-yard pass from Brister (Bahr PAT)
PHI—Hebron 1-yard run (Bahr PAT)
NYJ—Safety, Brister called for intentional grounding in end zone
PHI—Allen 94-yard interception return (Bahr PAT)

Eric Allen

Here's all you need to know about Eric Allen. He intercepted 54 passes and returned eight of them for touchdowns in his 14-year NFL career.

Allen combined an unparalleled work ethic, a brilliant football mind, and remarkable athleticism to become one of the greatest cornerbacks in NFL history. He played in six Pro Bowls and matched Bill Bradley's franchise record of 34 interceptions, a mark later tied by Brian Dawkins. He finished his career with the Saints and Raiders before becoming one of the most highly respected TV football analysts in the business.

"Eric was just a phenomenal athlete," longtime teammate Seth Joyner said. "Any time he got his hands on the ball, he had the intention of getting it into the end zone. He was truly a playmaker. He wasn't looking to go out of bounds, he was looking to score."

Even though Allen stood 5'10" and weighed just 180 pounds, the Eagles' massive defensive linemen considered him one of their own because of his toughness, his willingness to support the run, and his passion for hitting.

"I loved my time in Philly with those guys," Allen said. "If I'm ever able to get to the Hall of Fame, it'll be because of those guys who really pushed me and that fan base who didn't want anything less than your best. I had fun in New Orleans and Oakland, but I'll always be an Eagle."

Considered one of the great ball hawks of all time, Allen was also known as a smart player. His intelligence is apparent in his job as a football analyst on television.

January 11, 2004

Fourth-and-26

Last-Minute Fourth-Down Conversion Keeps Eagles Alive in Playoff Win Over Packers

The play clock kept ticking … 0:04 … 0:03 … 0:02 … and the Eagles scrambled to line up for the most important play of the season. The challenge they faced was already virtually impossible—and it was about to get even harder. Fourth-and-26 was about to turn into fourth-and-31.

"That wouldn't have been good," Donovan McNabb says now, laughing. "We really raced up to the line of scrimmage to get the ball snapped just to give ourselves an opportunity."

Once everybody was set—with one second showing on the clock—center Hank Fraley snapped the football to McNabb, starting one of the most improbable plays in NFL history.

The Eagles trailed Brett Favre and the Packers 17–14 with 72 seconds left in their 2003 playoff game at the Linc. The Eagles had battled back from a 14–0 deficit, but time was running out, they had no timeouts, and Packers cornerback Bhawoh Jue had just sacked McNabb for a 16-yard loss, back to the Eagles' 26-yard line.

"I'm thinking, *How the hell did we just lose 16 yards on one play?*" Ike Reese said. "I'll be honest. I thought the game was over."

McNabb threw incomplete to tight end Chad Lewis on third down, leaving the Eagles with a fourth-and-26. Convert or the season ends.

"All of us just had the mentality that we were going to get it done," McNabb said. "You don't want to think negative thoughts in a situation like that."

But what play do you call on fourth-and-26?

"As a defense, all you have to do is drop back to the sticks in a zone and let him catch the ball in front of you," Reese says now. "I'm thinking, *We don't even have anybody fast enough to get down the field in time for him to turn around and catch the damn ball before he gets sacked.*"

But Freddie Mitchell, who didn't have a catch in the game, knew he could get open.

"I didn't say anything to Donovan because he wasn't going to listen to me, but I told [receivers coach] David Culley, 'Dude, the middle has been open the whole game. Will you tell him I'm going to be wide open on this play?'"

Freddie Mitchell pumps his fist after catching a fourth-down pass for 28 yards late in the fourth quarter against the Green Bay Packers during their NFC playoff game on January 11, 2004. The Eagles won 20–17 in overtime.

Mitchell recalled. "Donovan said, 'You ready?' Am I ready? I've been ready all f--ing day."

Mitchell lined up to McNabb's right and got off a bump on the line of scrimmage from cornerback Michael Hawthorne. McNabb, who had already been sacked eight times in the game, had great protection this time and stood tall in the pocket.

"I thought back to the NFC Championship Game two years earlier in St. Louis, when we had fourth down at the end and Donovan threw to Freddie but they brought the house, Donovan didn't have much time, and then he got picked off," running back Duce Staley said. "So I thought the Packers were going to blitz everybody like the Rams did. But they didn't bring anybody, and Donovan had all day. *OK, we have a shot. Just find somebody.*"

McNabb fired.

"Donovan valued Freddie in clutch moments," Lewis said. "With the season on the line, he went to him."

Game Details

Philadelphia Eagles 20 • Green Bay Packers 17 (OT)

Eagles	0	0	7	10	**17**
Packers	14	0	0	0	**14**

Date: January 11, 2004

Team Records: Philadelphia 12–4, Green Bay 10–6

Scoring Plays:

GB—Ferguson 40-yard pass from Favre (Longwell PAT)

GB—Ferguson 17-yard pass from Favre (Longwell PAT)

PHI—Staley 7-yard pass from McNabb (Akers PAT)

PHI—Pinkston 12-yard pass from McNabb (Akers PAT)

GB—Longwell 21-yard FG

PHI—Akers 37-yard FG

PHI—Akers 31-yard FG

The ball sailed inches out of the reach of a lunging Bwawoh [Jue], and Mitchell leaped high at midfield, turned his body toward McNabb, reached straight out, and snagged the football.

"I just saw him running right down the middle and tried to put it in a position where he could compete for it," McNabb said.

Safeties Darren Sharper and Marques Anderson had both run beyond midfield, giving Mitchell room. Sharper blasted Mitchell from behind, but Mitchell not only held on but fell forward to the 48, two yards beyond the first-down line.

"If he could get open—*if* he could get open—Freddie was pretty strong around the ball," said Brad Childress, then the Eagles' offensive coordinator.

The 28-yard gain was Mitchell's longest in five weeks.

"It was about negative 30, and the ball was hard as hell," Mitchell said. "I was like, 'Man, I gotta catch this.' I stuck my hand out and it stuck to me. 'Just hold onto the ball.' I hit the ground and just started looking for the marker. 'Oh crap, it's close.'"

Close, but a first down—the longest fourth-down conversion in NFL postseason history.

"Maybe fourth-and-18," Staley said. "Maybe fourth-and-20. Maybe even fourth-and 22. But fourth-and-26? I couldn't believe it."

David Akers tied the game with a 37-yard field goal with five seconds left in the fourth quarter, then won it with a 31-yarder in overtime after Brian Dawkins intercepted Favre at the Packers' 35-yard line.

"I didn't have the numbers and I didn't have the Pro Bowls," Mitchell said. "But the fans look for memories. The media called me a bust, but there's a memory nobody can take away from me."

I'm thinking, *That did not just happen.*

—EAGLES RUNNING BACK DUCE STALEY

Donovan and Freddie

Donovan McNabb and Freddie Mitchell are linked together forever by two things. First, they connected on two of the greatest plays in Eagles history: fourth-and-26 and "the Play That Went on Forever." And second, they couldn't stand each other.

"They'd have their spats," Pro Bowl special teamer Ike Reese said. "Donovan would take all the receivers out and wouldn't invite Freddie. Donovan would have Thanksgiving or Christmas at his house and invite the offensive players over, wouldn't invite Freddie. It was crazy."

How did it start?

"I really have no idea," McNabb says now. "Some people, that's their deal. They throw negative attention off them and put it on someone else. When things are going bad, 'Well, it's not me, I'm running my route.'"

Mitchell was the opposite of McNabb, and the fans loved his colorful personality and provocative quotes.

"[McNabb] was jealous," Mitchell says today. "He hated the fact that the fans and the media loved me more than him. He only threw me the ball when he had to."

In September 2004, McNabb's wife Roxie gave birth to their first child, daughter Alexis.

"They had the baby shower, and Freddie bought them this expensive-ass stroller, a Bugaboo carriage. It was like a $500 stroller for a freaking infant," Reese said. "He went out to try and butter him up. We're in the cafeteria and Donovan said, 'This [guy] thinks because he bought my baby an expensive-ass stroller we're cool now?'"

Mitchell, drafted in the 2001 draft ahead of Reggie Wayne, Chad Johnson, and Steve Smith, started only 17 games, but he did provide something the other receivers didn't.

> **W**henever anyone says "fourth-and-26," they don't say "Donovan McNabb threw that pass." They say "Freddie Mitchell caught that pass."
>
> —EAGLES RECEIVER FREDDIE MITCHELL

"He was the toughest guy on our offense," Reese said. "But he wanted to be the flamboyant guy. That was his problem. He wanted to be the T.O., the Chad Johnson, as opposed to being the hard-hat guy. Bring the lunch pail, make all the tough catches, talk a little trash, let a defensive player know he ain't hurt you and you're coming back across the middle again. In this city? With this fan base? He would have been a media magnet."

Instead, he talked his way out of town. When Mitchell mocked the Patriots' secondary before the Super Bowl and then bashed McNabb after it, he was gone.

"He always thought he was more than what he was, and he carried himself that way, and for a while it was funny and then it became irritating," Reese said. "Come on, dude. You're still talking about what type of receiver you are, and reality says you're not that guy. I loved Freddie Mitchell. But that last year, he was just doing crap on purpose. He was really, in my opinion, trying to screw up our opportunity to win a ring. He didn't care."

Mitchell caught just 90 passes and never reached 500 yards in a season. He scored five touchdowns. He was out of the league soon after his 26th birthday.

"It's unfortunate, because he could have been a good player," McNabb said. "But it just didn't happen."

3

November 20, 1960

Bednarik KOs Gifford

Bednarik's Devastating Hit Knocks Out Gifford, Lifts Eagles to Crucial Win Over Giants

There was no reason to believe the 1960 Eagles were going to be all that different from the 1959 Eagles or 1958 Eagles—or any Eagles team from a decade that included few happy days. After winning their second consecutive NFL title in 1949, the Eagles spent the 1950s going from mediocre to worse. From 1950 through 1959, the Eagles averaged just five wins per year.

Then came 1960, a 6–1 start, and a crucial midseason game against the 5–1–1 Giants, the two-time defending Eastern Conference champions. The Eagles knew they had to beat the Giants to have a reasonable chance to win an NFL title.

"I don't think anyone thought we were going to beat the Giants," wide receiver Tommy McDonald said. "Nobody picked us to beat the Giants. Nobody but us."

That day at Yankee Stadium, the Eagles fought back from a 10–0 halftime deficit and took a 17–13 lead when Chuck Bednarik forced a Mel Triplett fumble. Jimmy Carr recovered it and returned it for a touchdown.

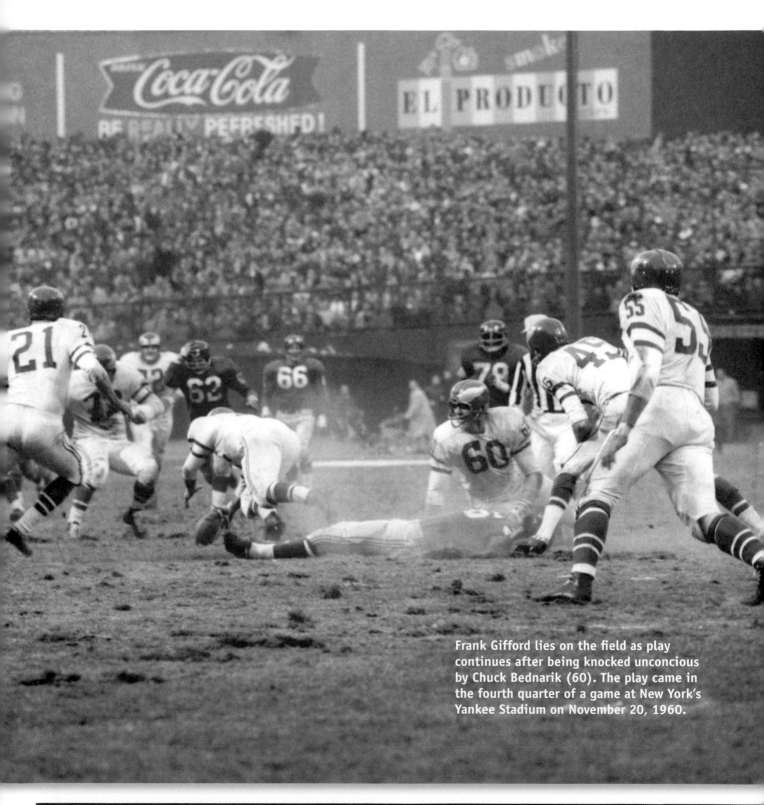

Frank Gifford lies on the field as play continues after being knocked unconcious by Chuck Bednarik (60). The play came in the fourth quarter of a game at New York's Yankee Stadium on November 20, 1960.

The Giants had one last chance, and on a key third-and-10 at midfield, quarterback George Shaw looked to his primary target, Frank Gifford.

"He was their guy," Bednarik said of Gifford, the star tailback from USC. "We all kind of knew they would go to him in that situation."

They went to him, although Gifford probably wishes they didn't. Gifford caught Shaw's pass at the Eagles 35, enough for a first down, and then attempted to cut back behind Bednarik, who was circling in coverage. Bad decision.

In one of the iconic moments in league history, Bednarik belted Gifford with a high, hard blindside hit so ferocious that it sent him crashing to the frozen turf unconscious. The ball came loose. Linebacker Chuck Weber recovered. The game was over.

The surprising Eagles improved to 7–1 on their way to the NFL title. Gifford had suffered a severe head injury and was done for the season. And the next season.

"It was perfectly legal," Gifford said years later. "If I'd had the chance, I would have done the same thing to Chuck."

Gifford returned to the Giants in 1962 as a wide receiver and played three more seasons, even making the Pro Bowl in 1963.

"It was a clean hit, clean all the way," Bednarik says now. "I just hit him high in the chest about as hard as I could. His head snapped and he went flying one way and the ball went flying the other. I was trying to follow the ball, so I didn't know what happened to Gifford. When I saw our linebacker Chuck Weber got the ball, I raised my hand in the air, because I knew we had won the game. I didn't know Gifford was lying there on the ground. I had no idea. I wasn't taunting him or any of that. I wouldn't do that. I was celebrating because I knew the game was over."

As the years pass by, the play, "the Hit," never goes away.

"I do those card shows, autograph shows, and someone always comes up with that picture for me to sign," Bednarik said of the famous shot of him standing over the fallen Gifford. "One time, a guy asked me, 'Mr. Bednarik, what were you saying right there?' I told him I said, 'This f––ing

game is over.' So now, they want me to write it explicitly, but I don't. I'll just literally write *This bleeping game is over* and sign it."

Bednarik gets a kick out of the fact that almost 50 years later people still want to talk about the hit. He thinks he knows why it's so popular.

"It happened in New York," he said. "I always tell people that if you do anything big, do it in New York. And second, since it happened to a revered guy like Frank, it will never die."

Bednarik has seen Gifford over the years. The conversations have been brief but cordial.

"There are no ill feelings," Bednarik said. "The one time I saw him, he joked with me. He told me he helped make me famous."

> **T**hat hit put the nail in the board. After that everyone knew the Philadelphia Eagles were for real. R-E-A-L, real.
>
> —EAGLES RECEIVER TOMMY McDONALD

Game Details

Philadelphia Eagles 17 • New York Giants 10

Eagles	0	0	7	10	**17**
Giants	7	3	0	0	**10**

Date: November 20, 1960

Team Records: Philadelphia 6–1, New York 5–1–1

Scoring Plays:

NYG—Morrison 1-yard run (Summerall PAT)

NYG—Summerall 28-yard FG

PHI—McDonald 35-yard pass from Van Brocklin (Walston PAT)

PHI—Walston 12-yard FG

PHI—Carr 38-yard fumble return (Walston PAT)

Concrete Charlie

If all had gone as planned, Chuck Bednarik wouldn't have even played football in 1960. He wouldn't have knocked out Frank Gifford or tackled Jim Taylor, and the Eagles almost certainly wouldn't have won the NFL Championship.

"We had an addition to the family, twins," he said. "So I decided I [had] better keep working."

Bednarik returned as a center, but because of injuries, he wound up playing center and linebacker, the NFL's last two-way player.

"I just played football," Bednarik said. "I think a lot of guys would have gone both ways if somebody asked. Nobody ever asked."

Bednarik made eight Pro Bowl teams and was named to the NFL's all-time team in 1994 and inducted into the Hall of Fame in 1967, his first year of eligibility.

"I would say he's the best to ever wear an Eagles uniform," NFL historian Ray Didinger said. "With a lot of players or plays, the legend grows as time passes. You know, 400-foot home runs become 600-foot home runs, or they say a guy broke 20 tackles and you watch it and he broke two. With Chuck, the legend doesn't even describe how good he was."

Bednarik finally retired for good after the 1962 season, his 14th year with the Eagles.

"Old No. 60, there will never be another one like him," fellow Hall of Famer Tommy McDonald says. "There was only one Chuck Bednarik. Nobody could ever fill his shoes. He just loved to play football. "That's all he wanted to do, play football."

To this day, Concrete Charlie epitomizes the hard-nosed brand of football still played by the Eagles.

2

January 11, 1981

"I've Never Heard It Louder"

Montgomery Overcomes Knee Injury to Lead Eagles to First Super Bowl

Three days before he scored one of the most historic touchdowns in Eagles history, Wilbert Montgomery couldn't walk. He couldn't even stand up.

"We were practicing in Tampa all week," Montgomery said. "I was running down the field, and my legs just gave out. It felt like somebody shot me. I was down for the count."

Montgomery, who had missed four games during the regular season with a hyperextended knee, was now in danger of missing the NFC Championship Game with a related injury.

"[Trainers] Otho [Davis] and Ron O'Neil worked on me the next few days," Montgomery said. "They packed me in ice and told me I needed to rest. On Sunday, I didn't even come out for pregame warm-ups. I was still inside for treatment. When the game started, Louie Giammona was our starting running back."

But inside, Montgomery was feeling better. Maybe he'd give it a try.

"We ran the first play, and then I came down the tunnel, and I'm standing on the sidelines, and I told Coach V [Dick Vermeil], 'I'm ready to go,'" he said. "He just looked at me and said, 'Get in there.'"

On second down, Vermeil lined up with three wide receivers, a formation the Eagles had thrown out of.

"We hadn't run out of that formation all year," Vermeil said. "So they sent their nickel package out there. They had six defensive backs. They never thought we'd run."

This time they did, and Dallas never recovered.

"It was supposed to be a run off the left side, between left tackle Stan Walters and left guard Petey Perot," Montgomery said. "But the hole opened up on the backside, where Petey got push on John Dutton. I was able to put my foot in the ground and make that cut. Next thing you know, I got to the second level, and I was able to score. They were playing the pass, and we tricked them. That was great blocking. All I did was run through the hole."

Montgomery's run was the longest in an NFC title game in 28 years, since Doak Walker of the Lions had a 67-yarder against the Browns in 1952. At the time, it was the longest postseason touchdown ever run against the Cowboys.

Eagles running back Wilbert Montgomery stiff arms safety Dennis Thurman (32) during the Eagles' 20-7 win over the Cowboys in the 1980 NFC Championship Game at the Vet. Montgomery rushed for 194 yards, including a historic 42-yard touchdown on his first carry of the game.

"He was in the end zone so fast," linebacker Bill Bergey said. "Before their defensive backs turned around, he was gone."

Even though the game was only 131 seconds old, everybody at the Vet could sense what was happening. The Eagles were on their way to the Super Bowl.

"The fans were electric," Montgomery said. "It was so loud after that play, it was just unbelievable. I've never heard it louder."

The Cowboys actually did tie the game in the second quarter on Tony Dorsett's three-yard touchdown run, but it didn't matter. The Eagles scored the game's final 13 points on a Leroy Harris touchdown run and two short Tony Franklin field goals to win 20-7 and advance to their first Super Bowl.

"They didn't have the respect for us that we deserved in that kind of game," Vermeil said. "I guess they felt they could whip our butts because we were the Eagles and they were the Cowboys. But we felt the only way we were inferior to them was if we believed it ourselves."

Despite being forced out of the game for a while in the second half when his legs gave out again, Montgomery rushed for 194 yards, which going into 2009 was still the 10th-highest total ever in an NFL playoff game.

But this was more than just a huge postseason win for the Eagles. This was a triumph of good over evil. The arrogant Dallas Cowboys and their Hall of Famers and their Super Bowl trophies came to Philadelphia to walk all over an Eagles team that had won two playoff games in 20 years. And two plays in, the Eagles had punched them in the face.

"I can honestly say walking through that tunnel before the game—and I think every Eagle player felt the same way—that I was thinking, *I wonder how bad we're going to beat these bastards*," Bergey said. "Dick Vermeil had us so well prepared. I don't think I've ever been so prepared for a football game in my life.

"The score was 20-7, but it could easily have been 35-3 or even worse. We literally beat the hell out of the Dallas Cowboys."

And it all began with a 42-yard touchdown run by a guy who couldn't walk a couple days earlier.

"That was America's team, and everybody in Philly hated them," Montgomery said. "They came in over-confident. Just before the game, coach Vermeil told us, 'We're going to kick the crap out of the Dallas Cowboys.' And that's just what we did."

I really had my doubts whether I'd be able to play on Sunday. I was hurting.

—EAGLES RUNNING BACK WILBERT MONTGOMERY

Game Details

Philadelphia Eagles 20 • Dallas Cowboys 7

Eagles	7	0	10	3	**20**
Cowboys	0	7	0	0	**7**

Date: January 11, 1981

Team Records: Philadelphia 12–4, Dallas 12–4

Scoring Plays:

PHI—Montgomery 42-yard run (Franklin PAT)

DAL—Dorsett 3-yard run (Septien PAT)

PHI—Franklin 26-yard FG

PHI—Harris 9-yard run (Franklin PAT)

PHI—Franklin 20-yard FG

Wilbert Montgomery

The Eagles had only three points to show for the first half, so at halftime of the Eagles' late-season game against the Giants in 1977, coach Dick Vermeil told rarely used rookie tailback Wilbert Montgomery he was starting the second half.

"I had been returning kicks, but I hadn't played on offense," Montgomery recalls. "I said, 'Coach, I haven't had a playbook since we were in training camp.'"

Vermeil didn't care. Montgomery took over, and the 23-year-old rookie sixth-round pick responded with 59 yards on 13 carries, 37 yards on the winning drive. The Eagles, who had won only three of their first 12 games, beat the Giants, 17–14.

Montgomery was on his way to greatness, and so were the Eagles. The Eagles hadn't reached the playoffs in 17 years, but with Montgomery leading the way, they reached the postseason four straight years, from 1978 through 1981. During that span, Montgomery averaged more than 1,200 rushing yards, 40 catches and nearly 1,500 yards of offense, and went to the Pro Bowl twice. When he retired, he ranked 13th in NFL history with 6,789 rushing yards.

"When Dick got to Philly in 1976, he weeded out the guys who didn't fit and looked for guys who put the team before themselves," Montgomery said. "We were a family. There wasn't one player on that team that didn't get along with everybody else on that team. We all pulled and cheered for each other. We had a bunch of unselfish players who just wanted to win."

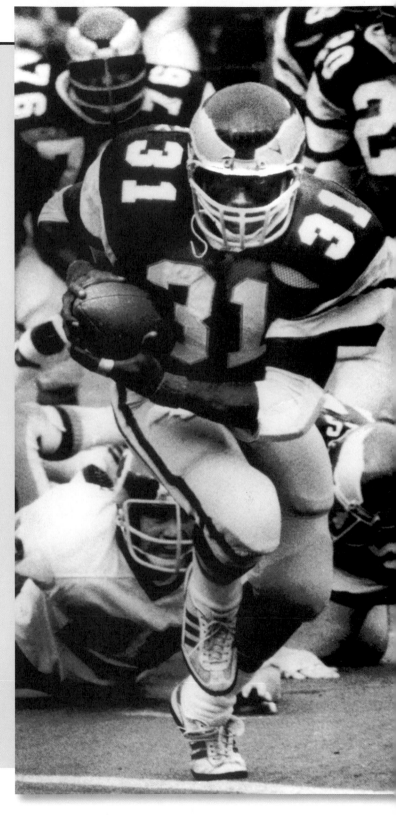

Running back Wilbert Montgomery blasts past Redskins safety Mark Murphy (29) on his way to 127 rushing yards during the Eagles' 28–17 win at the Vet in 1979.

October 10, 1988

The Ultimate Weapon

Cunningham Recovers from Certain Sack to Throw Miracle Touchdown

Carl Banks watched the play over and over for weeks, trying to figure out what he could have done differently. Finally, he just gave up.

"I actually made a good play," Banks said. "He just made a better play. It's like having your hand in the face of Michael Jordan, and he still makes the jumper. What are you going to do? I analyzed that play for two weeks straight after it happened to see if there was anything else I could have done. There wasn't."

The greatest play in Eagles history occurred during the team's first *Monday Night Football* game in seven years, when they hosted the Giants at Veterans Stadium in October 1988.

The Eagles trailed 3–0 with the ball at the Giants' 4-yard line early in the second quarter. Quarterback Randall Cunningham took the snap from center Dave Alexander and was immediately flushed out of the pocket.

He rolled to his right, and Banks was waiting. Banks, a 240-pound Pro Bowl linebacker, delivered a hit that sent Cunningham sprawling toward the ground back at the 10-yard line. It looked like a certain sack. But Cunningham refused to go down. He somehow maintained his balance, kept himself upright with his left hand, then straightened and, without pausing, fired a touchdown pass to tight end Jimmie Giles.

"I rolled around the corner, and I was really focused on the defense," Cunningham said. "Not many linebackers in that situation would come up like that, but Carl did. I was looking for Jimmie Giles the whole time, but he was covered. I knew if I could buy another second or two, he would get open.

"Carl hit me, and he hit me hard, knocked me off my feet. But I had that cat-like ability then. I was able to land on my feet, gain my balance, and, just as I thought, Jimmie got open in the end zone."

Cunningham made a living coming up with impossible plays. And that one was the most impossible of all.

"Was that my greatest play? I don't know," Cunningham says today. "I had some plays, I

Randall Cunningham, shown here taking on Giants defensive lineman John Washington on October 10, 1988, threw for 369 yards and three touchdowns in addition to pulling off the greatest play in Eagles history.

Randall

The miracles Randall Cunningham pulled off on game day were nothing compared to his miracles at practice.

"Randall could have been a Pro Bowl punter," teammate Garry Cobb said. "He could have been a Pro Bowl punt returner. He could have been a Pro Bowl wide receiver. He could have done anything he wanted to do. You would see him in practice just doing things that made you shake your head."

Buddy Ryan inherited a 23-year-old Cunningham when he became head coach in 1986 and gradually played him more and more until he was a full-time starter in 1987. By 1988, he was an MVP.

"I always said if I ever became a head coach I wanted a quarterback who could run and make plays," Ryan said. "I get to Philly and Randall's already there."

Cunningham took a lot of heat because he went 1–4 in the playoffs with the Eagles, but from 1987 through 1993, he threw 122 touchdowns to just 72 interceptions, went to three Pro Bowls, passed for more than 17,000 yards, rushed for more than 3,000, and compiled a 53–27 won–lost record. And he did it all despite playing behind ragtag offensive lines and without a big-time tailback or receiver.

"If they just would have put some more people around him, who knows what he would have done," Cobb said. "He did so much with so little.

"When you consider the way he played, how he changed the game, I think he definitely belongs in the Hall of Fame."

John Randall Cunningham demonstrated his exceptional athleticism not just on Sundays, but during the week at practice as well.

don't even know how I did them. Sometimes it was just divine intervention. And that certainly was one of them."

Mike Quick, the five-time Pro Bowl receiver, watched the game that night nursing a broken leg in the radio booth, where he would later become a fixture as the team's color analyst. Like everyone else, he couldn't believe what he saw.

"Randall looked like a superhero, Rubber Man, on that play," Quick said. "He stretched out, cut himself in half, and then popped back together and threw a touchdown pass."

The play wasn't only dazzling, it was important. It led to a 24–13 win on the way to the Eagles' first NFC East title since 1980.

"That just showed the kind of player Randall was and the great balance he had," coach Buddy Ryan said. "There wasn't much he couldn't do."

Even make a play like that while battling the flu.

"Nobody knew it, but I was sick that entire day," Cunningham said. "I had a temperature of about 102. I remember I told Buddy before the game I was sick. He said 'Don't worry, we'll sweat it out of you.' But I was half-groggy the whole game."

Groggy or not, Cunningham did what became routine for him: make truly unbelievable plays.

"The amazing thing about that play was that Randall was never concerned about the pressure," Eagles cornerback Eric Allen said. "He was so confident in his ability to escape from any situation that it just didn't matter to him. So once he's hit and he's off his feet, he just kept his vision and focused down the field.

"Any other quarterback would either have crumbled to the ground or run for his life, but nothing affected Randall. He was like, 'OK, here comes some pressure, no problem, I'm going to make this play.' That was such an unbelievable athletic play, but it just seemed so effortless for him. He just had this grace about him. He was like a puma, always smooth and powerful, and always calm."

Banks still shakes his head in disbelief when asked about the play.

"Any other player would have gone down," Banks said. "I didn't miss many tackles in my career. That was just a great play by him. And it just so happened it was on *Monday Night Football* for the world to see. The guy was unbelievable. He had that sixth sense, like he had eyes in the back of his head. But I loved playing against him. It was always a great challenge.

"We talk about [the play] all the time, every time I see him. I tell him how I made him famous and he owes me some of that endorsement money he made."

> **T**hat's the greatest play I've ever seen by an Eagle.
>
> —RECEIVER MIKE QUICK

Game Details

Philadelphia Eagles 24 • New York Giants 13

Eagles	0	14	3	7	**24**
Giants	3	0	3	7	**13**

Date: October 10, 1988

Team Records: Philadelphia 2–3, New York 3–2

Scoring Plays:

NYG—Allegre 47-yard FG

PHI—Giles 4-yard pass from Cunningham (Zendejas PAT)

PHI—Byars 5-yard pass from Cunningham (Zendejas PAT)

PHI—Zendejas 37-yard FG

NYG—Allegre 22-yard FG

NYG—Mowatt 38-yard pass from Simms (Allegre PAT)

PHI—Carter 80-yard pass from Cunningham (Zendejas PAT)